Pre-School

Transiti... the Earl... Years

A practical guide to supporting transitions between early years settings and into Key Stage One

by Sue Allingham

Contents

Published by Practical Pre-School Books, A Division of MA Education Ltd, St Jude's Church, Dulwich Road, Herne Hill, London, SE24 0PB.

Tel: 020 7738 5454

www.practicalpreschoolbooks.com

© MA Education Ltd 2011

All images © MA Education Ltd., other than the images listed below.

Front cover images (clockwise from top left): © iStockphoto.com/microgen, © iStockphoto.com/Steve Debenport, © iStockphoto.com/Claudia Dewald, © iStockphoto.com/Rosemarie Gearhart, © iStockphoto.com/Brittney McChristy, © iStockphoto.com/Miroslav Ferkuniak.

All photos other than the above taken by Ben Suri.

ISBN 978-1-907241-19-2

Early Childhood Essentials

Understanding transitions

Supporting and understanding transitions

Everyone feels comfortable

This book is for everybody who works with children. Early transitions affect not just those working in the early years – from birth to five – but also those working beyond that and into primary school. A list of the adults involved in transitions in the early years must include:

- Teachers (see the broad definition in the glossary on page 5)

- Administration staff

- Visiting adults, such as photographers, and specialists who teach music, dance, French etc.

- Adults from other agencies. For example, health visitors, school nurses, early years advisory teams, speech therapists, and physiotherapists

- Assessors visiting adults who are training in early years work

- Students

- Kitchen staff

- Parent helpers and volunteers

Defining a 'transition': key messages

The key messages in this book are aimed at supporting children and adults to cope with transitions both between and within settings – these practical ideas will be valuable to all who work with children and families – in whatever capacity or setting, and at whatever stage of development.

In this book I define transition as any kind of change that may alter the routines that the children, and sometimes the adults, are used to. This does not just mean moving from room to room or between settings. The change can also be something as simple as the introduction of a new staff member, a staff member leaving, an unexpected visitor to the group, or someone different bringing the child to, or collecting them from, the setting.

These key messages are not dependent upon a particular curriculum or national education system as, wherever you are based, there is a need to have an understanding of how children, and adults, can be supported in coping with the potential issues around transition. This is particularly important to be aware of at a time when policies and guidance are under review. The messages in this book have their roots in respected research and good practice.

Different curricula

Being aware of, and managing appropriately, the effect that transition events may have on the feelings of the children in our settings is central to supporting them. It is important to note that, whatever curriculum you are working from, the documents that you have will be in agreement with, and support, the thinking that this book will encourage. This is because each curriculum document recognises the need for consistency across each stage of learning. The section below illustrates the focus that each of the early years curricula from the four governments in the United Kingdom places on transitions.

Key supporting points from The Early Years Foundation Stage

This document is an amalgam of previous documents with the purpose of promoting continuity from birth to five and supporting "children's learning and development and welfare" (DCSF, 2008, page 5). The EYFS clearly identifies that children will be educated in a variety of settings:

> Many children will receive education and care under the EYFS framework in more than one setting. Some may attend part-time, while others may attend full-time and also use extended services, such as breakfast or after-school clubs. These patterns of attendance will be a key factor in planning. For children who attend more than one setting, practitioners must ensure effective continuity and progression by sharing relevant information with each other and parents. (EYFS (2008) *Statutory Framework for the Early Years Foundation Stage*, DCSF, page 6)

The suggestions made here, such as continuity and sharing information with parents, will be discussed in subsequent chapters in this book.

Key supporting points from the Welsh curriculum

The Welsh Government revised their national curriculum to develop more consistency between the different phases of early education:

> The Foundation Phase is based on the principle that early years provision should offer a sound foundation for future learning through a developmentally appropriate curriculum. It will bring more consistency and continuity to children's education at such an all-important period in their development. (http://wales.gov.uk/topics/educationandskills/earlyyearshome/foundation_phase/?lang=en)

The Welsh Foundation Phase runs from the ages of three to seven. In this way the stage incorporates what teachers in England would see as Key Stage One, and thus a more formal curriculum. The underpinning ethos is that:

> Practitioners should acknowledge prior learning and attainment, offer choices, challenge children with care and sensitivity, encourage them and move their learning along. Through careful observation and interaction with children, practitioners should focus on their achievements and development along a learning continuum. Observation is an integral part of the planning process. Future planning is based on their prior attainment and current achievements.

Observation and assessment enables practitioners to:

● know the individual child and highlight the child's strengths, interests and needs to identify the plan for the child's progress

● highlight the child's strengths and abilities across all areas of development and intelligences

● provide a graduated response and specific help to children whose progress is not adequate and who may be on the continuum of special educational needs (Welsh Assembly Government, Special Educational Needs Code of Practice for Wales, 2004)

- inform children, staff, parents/carers of children's achievements and the next steps in their learning

- identify, monitor and evaluate the effectiveness of the curriculum provided

- inform transition/transfer during the Foundation Phase, as well as between the Foundation Phase and Key Stage 2 (Welsh Assembly Government (2009) *Foundation Phase Child Development Profile Guidance*, Department for Children, Education, Lifelong Learning and Skills, page 2).

Key supporting points from the Scottish curriculum

The Scottish Curriculum for Excellence includes a guidance document called 'Pre-school into Primary Transitions' which states that "It has always been recognised that the transition from pre-school to primary school is a critical time of change for children, parents and practitioners – which is full of opportunity and potential" (Learning and Teaching Scotland, 2010, page 5). There is recognition that, "[t]he impact of transitions in the early years can strongly influence a child's future progress and development" (Learning and Teaching Scotland, 2010, page 6).

The 'Pre-school into Primary Transitions' guidance states that well-supported transitions can provide opportunities for:

- meaningful and challenging learning experiences

- new positive identities

- broadening horizons

- collaborative working

- strong relationships to be formed

- families to be meaningfully involved

- children to develop both emotionally and socially (Learning and Teaching Scotland, 2010, page 6)

The links between all stages of learning and the importance of understanding transitions are emphasised. Transitions offer opportunities for children to learn how to manage change in a positive way – an important skill to develop for life in the 21st century. Many practitioners across Scotland are capitalising on the opportunities opened up by Curriculum for Excellence to consider and enhance their current transitions practice.

Key supporting points from the Northern Ireland curriculum

The Northern Ireland Curriculum Primary document states that "children learn best when learning is connected".

Developing socially

Strong relationships

At Key Stages 1 and 2, to assist teachers in managing and making connections, each Area of Learning contains a paragraph highlighting the links to the rest of the curriculum.

Teachers should work together at a whole school level to ensure:

- the overall programme of learning in any one year group, and across the key stages, is broad and balanced

- there is continuity and progression in children's learning (Council for the Curriculum Examinations and Assessment, 2007, pages 10-11)

Conclusion

Each of the documents outlined above from the four UK governments place a strong emphasis on the importance of continuity across the age range from birth to seven. For this to happen, it is very important that the process of transition is considered thoroughly and that children move through settings where like-minded people provide appropriate experiences.

The purpose of this book is to examine the implications and effects of transition.

- In chapter one key documents will be examined to develop the idea of why transitions are increasingly recognised as issues that need addressing

- In chapter two the ideas of transition and change and the impact they may have on families and children will be discussed

- In chapter three five case studies drawn from different types of settings will be used to identify points of transition and show how they can be dealt with sensitively

- chapter four is to be used to as a discussion point, to support team meetings, to review provision and to develop useful policies

How to use this book

Each chapter begins with two bullet points

- A statement or question to keep in mind and reflect upon as the chapter unfolds

- How each chapter links to the policy documents mentioned above

At the end of each chapter there is a set of questions that are designed to be used as a basis for team meetings and reflection on practice. The final chapter contains proforma which can be used in this process, along with examples of policy statements to support settings to develop their own documents.

GLOSSARY

Parent: for the purposes of this book the term 'parent' covers any adult who is acting in a parental role for the child.

Setting: this term is used to cover any environment that children attend away from their own home. This includes the home of a childminder, or a school.

Teacher: throughout this book the term 'teacher' is used to refer to all adults who work with young children and plan for their learning. In this way the term is used much more broadly than the definition of Qualified Teacher Status and covers the range of adults that children and their families will meet in each setting they access.

Chapter 1

What is transition?

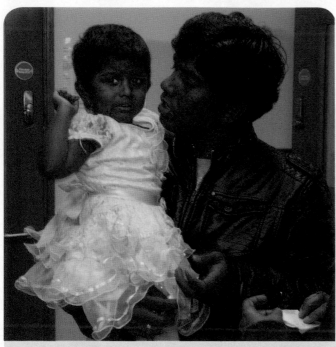

Transitions to a new setting can be upsetting

A shared understanding from early years into school

As you read this chapter, reflect on:

- How do you feel when something new happens, or you are in a new situation? What do you do? What helps?

Key references

Recognising that children potentially face a number of transitions in their early lives is key in each of the early years guidance documents in Great Britain. For example:

- The Early Years Foundation Stage states that "for children who attend more than one setting, practitioners must ensure effective continuity and progression by sharing relevant information with each other and parents" (DCSF

(2008) *Practice Guidance for the Early Years Foundation Stage*, page 6)

- The Welsh Learning and Teaching Pedagogy document emphasises the importance of "children's pre-school experiences on their subsequent development" (Welsh Assembly Government, 2008, page 5)

- The Scottish document, *Curriculum for Excellence: Pre-school into Primary Transitions* emphasises the need for "practitioners across the pre-school and primary sectors are developing a better shared understanding" (The Scottish Government, 2008, page 5)

- The Northern Irish document, *Understanding the Foundation Stage* notes that "Young children come to school from a variety of different backgrounds, having had a range of diverse learning experiences at home and for most, some form of pre-school education" (Northern Ireland Curriculum, 2006, page 1)

The present situation

We are at a time when there is a national focus on early years provision – both on practice and the impact it makes on future learning. Whilst this is a good thing, it can mean that there is a danger of losing sight of the practice because we are focussing on the impact; for example how the children will achieve academically at the end of the next Key Stage. Pressure put on the curriculum can make it easy to forget that we are working with the very youngest children and everything we do with them and for them has an impact of its own. Going through transitions is something that we as adults, who are also children's teachers at this crucial stage, may take in our stride, but we need to understand the implications these events may have in order to give support and guidance.

The aim of this book is to be a practical resource to aid teachers in their reflection on how children are supported through transition. In Liz Brooker's title, *Starting School: Young Children Learning Cultures*, she explores the impact of transition:

> I used to be a Reception teacher, and for twenty years or so I thought of myself, with some reservations, as a good one. The reservations were there because although I managed, on the whole, to help four-year-olds from a variety of backgrounds to adapt successfully to school learning, there were always a few children for whom my professional practice didn't seem to work. These children – looking back, they tended to be mostly either from the Bangladeshi community, or from the poorest white families – spent two years in my class without noticeably latching on to learning. Perhaps all teachers have this experience. (Brooker, 2002, page ix)

Brooker realised that the transition to school was not the same for every child; she describes it as "developmentally dramatic" (Brooker, 2002, page ix) because it often involves changes for children that none of their previous experiences could have prepared them for. She has since been involved in other work in this area. Some of which will be referred to throughout this book.

As seen at the start of this chapter, the concept of supporting children through transition is increasingly featuring in documents and guidance. The fact that there was an issue around transition first came to the attention of teachers after the *Curriculum*

Guidance for the Foundation Stage (QCA, 2000) was introduced. Although there had previously been The Desirable Outcomes for Children's Learning (SCAA, 1996) which outlined six areas of learning but gave very little support towards teaching, this new document was the first time there had been a comprehensive guidance for those working in the early years. As a result of this, the differences between the two curriculums, from early years into Key Stage One, became clear and the two stages were perceived to be very different. Until this point the idea that children may find moving through the different years of school difficult had not really been considered. The philosophy of the new Foundation Stage, with its 'areas of learning', progress marked out in practical steps, and emphasis on 'appropriate' learning, highlighted differences to the potentially more 'formal' ways of working in Key Stage One. Tensions arose. This resulted in a National Foundation for Educational Research document entitled, *A Study of the Transitions from the Foundation Stage to Key Stage One* (Sanders et al, 2005) to consider how children and adults felt about the move into year one, and what might be done. Their findings reinforced that there were issues around transition for children, staff, and parents. Of particular relevance to this book are the following findings:

- Teachers said that they were able to manage the transition, but felt that some areas remained problematic. The biggest challenge was posed by the move from a play-based approach in the Foundation Stage to a more 'structured' curriculum in Key Stage One.

- School staff thought that children needed certain skills in order to make a good start in year one. These included: being able to care for themselves and to carry out tasks without adult support, an ability to listen to the teacher, and to sit still.

- While staff thought that most children coped well with the transition to year one, certain children were identified as more likely to experience problems. These included children who were younger, or less mature, less able, had special educational needs or spoke English as an additional language.

- Parents wanted more information about transition. They wanted to know what would be expected of their children, so they could help them prepare for year one. They would have liked to meet their child's new teacher before the beginning of year one.

- The case-study schools had adopted a variety of strategies aimed at smoothing transition. These tended to focus on three areas: induction of children into year one, continuity of practice between reception and year one;

and communication between staff, parents and children. (Sanders et al, 2005)

Broadly speaking these issues can be summed up as covering these areas:

- Teachers felt that they could manage transition, but were holding on to the idea of a "play-based" curriculum, and a more "structured" one

- Year one teachers wanted children to be more independent, whilst at the same time needing them to be able to "listen to the teacher and to sit still"

- There is recognition that some children experience problems. There is a resonance here with Brooker's "reservations"

- Parents need to be involved and supported at times of transition Some settings had begun to understand and address these issues by focussing on continuity

There are then issues around well- being and involvement, differing expectations, misunderstandings – particularly in the thinking around preparing children for school, and working with parents. Chapters two and three of this book will look in greater detail at how these tensions and dichotomies of thinking might be overcome by looking at how provision can support transition by allowing all involved to feel comfortable. Chapter three illustrates this through five case studies.

Unfortunately many, if not all, of these issues, are still present today. This is despite the fact that in 2003 the then government published Excellence and Enjoyment: A Strategy for Primary Schools (DfES, 2003) which stated their aim to develop continuity between all stages of learning, to "make sure that children are supported at points of transfer and transition, especially as they move into primary school and as they move on to secondary".

The focus of the transition debate has tended to be around the move from the early years into Key Stage One and the differences between the two stages. The authors of the NFER (Sanders et al, 2005) research identify transition as a process of "adaptation", but their focus was only on the move into Key Stage One. That this transition was high in national thinking was further reinforced by the publication of Continuing the Learning Journey (QCA, 2005). This was published to support governors, senior leadership teams and teachers to understand how the move into Key Stage One could be done effectively.

Continuing the learning journey is a training package which builds upon the work which is already taking place in many schools to improve provision in the foundation stage. The package has been designed to help schools to give children a positive experience of transition as they move into Key Stage One and to show how to make most effective use of the information which comes from the foundation stage. (QCA, 2005, page 1)

The focus of this document was on learning from key features of good early years practice, and encouraging staff further up the school to value this and take it on in their own work in order to provide continuity.

However, as has been defined in the introduction of this book, there are far more permutations of transition. At the time Continuing the Learning Journey was written, The Curriculum Guidance for the Foundation Stage covered only the ages from three to five. There was a parallel document – Birth to Three Matters (DfES, 2002) – to support learning for younger children. This document was presented in a very different way from the Curriculum Guidance, and this in its own way created tensions. Because of this, thinking then moved forward and, after a consultation, the Early Years Foundation Stage was produced. This drew together Birth to Three Matters (DfES, 2002) and the Curriculum Guidance for the Foundation Stage (QCA, 2000). This new document made the differences even more sharply focussed with its clear principles, structure, and the fact that it is a statutory document for all adults who work with children ranging in age from birth to five.

However, Brooker (2008) states:

As the Early Years Foundation Stage is launched in England, children's daily lives will be regulated by Ofsted from shortly after their birth until they are 18 or older. Far from continuity, this provision could see them shift from daycare to pre-school and from nursery to reception class; from foundation stage unit to primary school, from primary to secondary, and from secondary to tertiary college. How many transitions is that? More importantly, are all these transitions planned and supported, or are some abrupt and scary? And what impact do they have on children's development and learning, their identity formation and their social competence? (Brooker, 2008, page 4)

Brooker also led research into "practitioners' experiences of the Early Years Foundation Stage" (DfE, 2010, page 1). One of the principal findings of this research report was that, though "practitioners broadly welcome improvements to continuity in the guidance", it was found that:

> For many children, the move from nursery into reception class and from reception to year one, involve significantly different experiences of ratios, routines, environments and pedagogy. (DfE, 2010, page 2)

The report identifies that:

> The majority of children living in England begin to attend group care settings long before they are three years old, and many experiences several settings in one week. (DfE, 2010, page 11)

A dictionary definition of 'transition' is:

> *Change* or passage from one state or stage to another; The period of time during which something changes from one state or stage to another; a *linking passage* between two divisions in a composition; bridge. (Collins English Dictionary, 2007).

I have italicised the word change as it is key to understanding the issues that arise at times of transition between settings, in varying degrees, for all children. The phrase "a linking passage" is also helpful to keep in mind as, for the children, transition is both a link and a passage – this is why there needs to be a focus on both continuity and progression at these times. Running a thesaurus search on the word 'change' through the computer brings up the words: alter, modify, vary, transform, revolutionise, adjust, and amend. When you consider the number of settings very young children may move through, sometimes daily, this change in setting must be balanced against the fact that they have very little life experience to help them to modify, adjust or amend their thinking and behaviour when faced with new situations. Brooker writes that transition "has been a recognized characteristic of human lives" (Brooker, 2008, page 2), and we all go through transitions of varying kinds throughout our lives. These are to do with growing up, forming relationships, developing careers, having children, and moving house. As we grow older we accept and deal with these things as they arise. Brooker points out however, that in modern times children have increasingly different experiences:

> In modern, complex societies, such events [transitions] are more frequent and perhaps less regarded: as the dissolution and reconstitution of families becomes more common, society may appear to pay little attention to the lives of individuals. But for those involved, and especially for the youngest children, they may overturn all the predictability and security of daily life and make the world seem an unsafe and frightening place. Disruptions to relationships occur against a background of other changes: families move home more

Year one children learning independently

Independent creativity in year one

So many transitions can be daunting

Familiar photographs allow the child to feel more settled

often, parents change jobs more often, *and children may have multiple changes of caregiver*. (Brooker, 2008, page 3)

I have italicised the last sentence as these "multiple changes of caregiver" could take place in one day, or over a week. Against this kind of scenario, settings may receive children who have experienced more disruption and discontinuity "than their professional caregivers have experienced in the course of their own lives" (Brooker, 2008, page 3). It is the responsibility of those working with the youngest children to be aware of this discrepancy between their own experiences as a child, and those of the children they care for. And it is the aim of this book to show how transitions can be managed without disruption and discontinuity.

Whilst the Early Years Foundation Stage aims to be supportive of the individual child and in this way will support transition between settings as it promotes continuity, this cannot be written without noting the recent Department for Education report (August 2010) which states:

> One of the intentions of the EYFS was to provide children with smoother transitions on the journey from home, through the pre-school years and into formal schooling. The many policy initiatives undertaken since 1997, all of them intended to improve the quality of early childhood experiences, are now seen, paradoxically, as increasing the number of transitions

children make in the years from birth to 5 (Brooker 2008). (DfE, 2010, pages 10-11)

Having established that children may go through disruption and discontinuity, transitions, as part of their home lives, it is important to establish what is meant by 'transition' in an early years context. The DfE research report states that practitioners are concerned about the number of transitions children make at different times in their first five years. These include:

● 'Horizontal' transitions between settings within the week or within the day, for children under three who, as a result of the greatly expanded provision of services in children's centres, attend childminders, drop-ins and stay and plays

● Transitions from the first caregivers (childminders or pre-schools, or both) into maintained nursery provision, between the ages of two and three

● Transitions from nursery provision into the reception class

● Transition from reception into year one (DfE, 2010, page 51)

The report notes that practitioners regard the transition from reception to year one as the most challenging. This is interesting and, as chapter three will show, studies of different types of provision show that this is not the case for those interviewed. Thus, for the purposes of this book, transition is viewed in broader terms and, although the move into year one is included, each transition is viewed as potentially challenging. In this way 'transition' is seen in this book as:

- From home to childminder

- From home to non-maintained setting

- Between non-maintained settings

- From room to room in a day nursery as children grow older

- From non-maintained setting to maintained nursery or school

- From home to maintained nursery

- From home to full-time school

- From maintained nursery to full-time school

- From the Foundation Stage (reception class or foundation stage unit) to Key Stage One

- From home to Key Stage One

This list is a stark reminder of what children of only a few weeks or months of age can go through – it is entirely likely that permutations of any of the first five on the list are happening daily to some very young children who pass through our settings. And that is not taking into account the number of different members of the family, friends, au pairs or nannies that may take the child to and from settings depending on which day or week it is.

Nutbrown and Page point out:

> Transitions have to happen in life, and young children experience many transitions in their first few years. But it is the practitioner's responsibility to really tune into the needs of the children and to take their cues from them. (Nutbrown and Page, 2008, page 137)

Both the Department for Education's recommendations, and Nutbrown and Page's research, focus on the wellbeing and comfort of the children as essential in supporting transition. However, it is not just the children that need to feel comfortable. The staff team also needs to have a shared understanding and vision of practice.

It is important for the staff team to review the children that they have in the setting to establish how many transitions they are going through and what these are. When this is done, look at how the children, families and even the staff team are supported to deal with these changes. It is important to realise that change affects everyone, not just the children.

Support from key documents

Having established a broad overview and definition of 'transition', it is important to recognise other key documents that underpin the importance of recognising the needs of the child. These should inform any approach to supporting the wellbeing of children at all times, including that of transition.

United Nations Rights of the Child

The Scottish Government's Early Years Framework quotes from the United Nations Rights of the Child document in its vision statement, and this UN document should underpin all work done with children as it is important that their rights are recognised. The Rights of the Child came into force in September 1990 and there are some articles that must be considered as important to transition. In particular:

- Article 3
  1. In all actions concerning children, whether undertaken by public or private social welfare institutions, courts of law, administrative authorities or legislative bodies, the best interests of the child shall be a primary consideration.

- Article 29
  1. States Parties agree that the education of the child shall be directed to:

  a) *The development of the child's personality, talents and mental and physical abilities to their fullest potential.*

- Article 31
  1. States Parties recognise the right of the child to rest and leisure, to *engage in play and recreational activities appropriate to the age of the child and to participate freely in cultural life and the arts.* (http://www.unhchr.ch/html/menu3/b/k2crc.htm)

I have italicised certain words in each article because for these developments and activities to happen teachers must be, what Nutbrown and Page called, really tuned in to the children they are working with. When transitions are not dealt with sensitively children can sometimes miss out on developing to their fullest potential, or stop enjoying free participation in recreation.

Every Child Matters

This document was published as a direct result of the Laming Report into the death of Victoria Climbie. It was put together with a view to stopping any child suffering in the future. Five outcomes were proposed to underpin all future thinking about provision – these were developed after consultation with children. Of relevance here are:

- Being healthy: enjoying good physical and mental health and living a healthy lifestyle

- Enjoying and achieving: getting the most out of life and developing broad skills for adulthood

- Making a positive contribution: to the community and to society and not engaging in anti-social or offending behaviour (HMSO, 2003, page 14)

These statements are important to the theme of transition because they encompass developing a well rounded child who is able to deal with situations and feels supported. The child who grows up to make a positive contribution to society will be the child whose wellbeing has been supported and has developed resilience. See chapter two of this book for more information on wellbeing.

Childcare Act 2006

It was the Childcare Act that established the development of the Early Years Foundation Stage. It was also this act that emphasised the importance of emotional wellbeing and put it high on both local and national agendas. It opens with the statement that it is to:

> Make provision about the powers and duties of local authorities and other bodies in England in relation to the improvement of the wellbeing of young children; (HMSO, 2006, page 1)

In the Childcare Act, achieving 'wellbeing' is related to:

a) Physical and mental health and emotional wellbeing
b) Protection from harm and neglect
c) Education, training and recreation
d) The contribution made by [children] to society
e) Social and economic wellbeing
(HMSO, 2006, page 1)

The emphasis on wellbeing is crucial to any thinking about transitions, and the fact that an Act of Parliament states that local authorities must improve the wellbeing of young children allows thinking and reflection on types of early provision that had started to be lost in more curriculum-biased agendas. Chapter two covers wellbeing in more depth.

KEY POINTS IN WHAT IS TRANSITION

Each of the documents outlined in this chapter puts the child firmly in the centre of any thinking around its care and education. Children's wellbeing must come first. At this point in your reading you should start making an action plan as to how you intend to review your provision with a view to supporting transition.

- Were you and your team aware of the key documents outlined above?

- If so, how are they reflected in your provision?

- If you were not aware of them, how will reading this chapter change your thinking? Are there key things that you will need to consider?

List the points that you will take forward in your thinking and keep them with you as you read the rest of this book.

Chapter 2

Feeling comfortable

As you read this chapter, reflect on:

- A situation, or group, where you feel comfortable. Why do you feel like that? How do you know? Conversely, think of situations or places where you feel uncomfortable and consider why this is so. If you don't have to, do you revisit these situations? And if you do, what are your coping strategies?

- How do other members of the team feel?

References from key documents

The Early Years Foundation Stage (DCSF, 2008) was developed as a direct recommendation of the Childcare Act 2006 In this way it reflects the emphasis put on wellbeing and emotional security:

> You must promote positive attitudes to diversity and difference within all children. In doing this you will help them to learn to value different aspects of their own and other people's lives. This includes making sure that all children and families feel included, safe and valued; that all children and adults are treated as individuals and are not discriminated against; and that all children are listened to and respected. (DCSF, 2008, page 6)

The Welsh Learning and Teaching Pedagogy document (Welsh Assembly Government, 2008) includes as some of its aims that children:

- Enjoy the best possible physical and mental, social and emotional health, including freedom from abuse, victimisation and exploitation

- Are listened to, treated with respect, and are able to have their race and cultural identity recognised

Sitting comfortably

- Have a safe home and a community that supports physical and emotional wellbeing (Welsh Assembly Government, 2008, page 3)

The Scottish document Curriculum for Excellence (The Scottish Government, 2008) is underpinned by the United Nations Rights of the Child (see chapter one). The government has also produced a guidance document for those working in early years entitled Active Learning in the Early Years (Scottish Executive, 2007).

- How do you support children to build relationships and become accustomed to new environments?

- How do you plan an environment and climate where children feel safe and confident to tackle new challenges and take risks, and where trial and error are viewed as a normal part of the learning process?

Feeling comfortable

In what ways do you provide an environment and ethos that encourages a positive sense of self and others, and respects diversity?
(Scottish Executive, 2007, page 9)

The Northern Irish document, *Understanding the Foundation Stage* points out that children learn best when they:

- Develop secure relationships with peers and adults;

- Have choice and exercise autonomy and independence in their learning, and are encouraged to take risks.

It also suggests that learning is supported by adults when:

- positively affirming environments are created to support children's emotional, social and physical development;
(Northern Ireland Curriculum, 2006, page 4)

Key words

Reading the extracts from national guidance above, certain key words and phrases show a common theme, which relates back to the end of chapter one and the key elements of early years practice that will support successful transitions. For times of transition to be smooth, supported, exciting and positive it is very important to be aware of the following qualities:

- positive attitudes

- diversity and difference

- safety

- valuing

- individuals

- listening

- respect

- cultural identity

- physical and emotional wellbeing

- building relationships

- confidence

- feeling safe to take risks

- positive sense of self and others

- secure relationships

- autonomy

- independence

- positively affirming environments

If all of these qualities are recognised in settings then children will be well prepared for transitions and life situations.

What to be aware of

It is clear from the statements from the UK national governments that the personal, social and emotional health of young children is of high priority in curriculum documents. The aim of this chapter is to highlight this thinking and develop key strands to use as a focus. Chapter three will then show how the strands are demonstrated in settings by using case studies drawn from a variety of early years settings. Focussing on the importance of personal, social and emotional development in this chapter is also intended to promote the fact that it must be an effective underpinning upon which to reflect when planning anything with children, of any age.

The children outlined here are children I've written about before. They are based on some I've met or heard about, but they are not unusual. It is useful to consider each of them and how the adults learnt to support them. What might have helped them though the transition into reception?

Child A was interesting right from the minute the teachers did their home visit. He lived in a small modern house that was immaculate and, unless you knew otherwise, you would never have known that four children lived there. There were no toys or children's things downstairs. 'A' wanted his visitors to see his room. He shared this with his older brother, but it contained only the beds, a large television and several toy cars. 'A' had lined the toy cars up neatly along the edge of the rug. 'A's' older brother and sister already attended the school and were known by the visiting teachers. He also had a baby brother who was in his mother's arms all through the visit.

Positively affirming environments are important

Feeling safe to take risks

In this environment 'A' appeared to be calm and well behaved. When he started at school, however, things were very different. He could not control himself, wouldn't listen and was very disruptive. The only person he would respond to positively in any way was his older sister. 'A' had not been to any type of pre-school.

Child 'B' started in the same class as 'A' at the same time. His mother did not want a home visit and this decision was respected by the practitioners. The family were refugees and there was no father present. On entry to school, 'B' showed very similar behaviour to 'A' and, although they competed with each other, it was often the two of them against the world as the other children did not like their activities destroyed. They were able to play alongside, but not with, each other. Child 'B' had also not been to a pre-school.

With both of these boys in the same room clear plans needed to be made to minimise disruption. Circle times were introduced using puppets to encourage talking and turn taking. Hand signals and pictures were used to gain attention quietly. Positive reinforcement was used instead of reprimands. The adults developed games to be played in small groups to promote turn taking and celebrate success. The day child 'A' and child 'B' were noted playing outside with the train together for a concentrated period was a breakthrough.

Child 'C' was very tall for his age. When he started in Reception it quickly became clear that his behaviour was different from the others. He often hit or bumped into children by mistake and, as a result was upset when they cried or were annoyed. He would also suddenly make loud crowing noises or call out. It didn't take long for the others to copy him.

When the teacher approached the parents with her concerns they were relieved that she had spoken to them. It transpired that their son had been 'expelled' from two playgroups as he had deemed to be 'naughty'. To hear that another professional was concerned and wanted to help was a huge relief for them. They took him to get some specialist advice and he was diagnosed with dyspraxia.

The staff took advice from his parents and started to use the gross motor activities that he had been given to develop his control. These were used as part of the physical work with the whole class.

Child 'D' was a selective mute. When she came to school she would only speak to her family or children of her own age. The staff wanted to be able to converse with her, but didn't push this as they knew that she could speak quite happily. They realised that it was a matter of biding their time. A firm relationship was built up with 'D' and her mother who became a class helper.

Feeling comfortable

This enabled the teachers to gain clear indicators of 'D's' achievements as she worked with her mother. Eventually she began speaking to the other adults quite naturally. She went through a mute phase again when she started in year one. Child 'D' had not been to pre-school.

Child 'E' was a little girl who had trouble getting to and from school as a parent had agoraphobia. This meant she was often late to arrive and to be collected. An informal arrangement developed between the parents and the staff that this would happen, and that if the parent needed to, she could stay and help in the class rather than go back outside until she felt comfortable. Child 'E' had not been to pre-school.

Child 'F' was a little boy who loved motorbikes. When the teachers visited him at home he was in the garden riding round on his own motorbike wearing his own set of leathers while his dad was working on a bike nearby. He excitedly showed his little bike to his visitors and they were very impressed with his knowledge.

When 'F' started in the reception class it became clear that his interests lay in constructing and creating. The Reception teachers were happy to feed this interest and develop it with relevant magazines and pictures. Child 'F' had not been to pre-school.

Once the teachers understood these children they were given the chance to 'fit in' and settle into their settings. However, this took some time, and the initial transitions were difficult to start with as the team had not, to begin with at least, considered the wellbeing of the children and how this period of transition would affect them.

How different would this have been if any of these children had been shouted at, made to sit on a 'naughty chair', been kept inside when they wanted to be outside, sent to the headteacher, or forced to do inappropriate activities. The list is endless but the negative results are easy to guess. Sadly all too often children are talked down to, ordered to do things or their feelings are completely ignored at home and in their settings. Unfortunately as some of the boys from the above examples progressed further through the school system they became disaffected as their wellbeing was increasingly disregarded. This resulted in two of them being excluded.

This reflection on the emotional environment must include the feelings of the adults as well. We can probably all remember a time of transition at some point in our lives that may or may not have gone very well. Reflecting on our own experiences and how we felt about them will enable us to better understand the children. Consider this reflection from one of the managers in the case studies:

I have gone through the process of thinking carefully about a transition in my life, and reflecting on how I coped, how I

Children need a chance to feel settled

Valuing individual interests is important

was helped, or could have been supported better to cope with the transition. It is worth the readers taking a moment and actually going through this process first. I fear some may read this without thinking about how a child FEELS through their transitions. In the same way the readers should think of a child or children who they don't feel is experiencing a smooth transition. This has made me think about my own transition to reception. We didn't have any nursery schools in the area, so it was straight from home to school. I initially went to a playgroup but I never settled in one – I screamed blue murder and pinned myself to my Dad's jacket.

I was scared of leaving my parents thinking that they might not be together when I got back, or be fighting without me being there to make sure they were ok. So I screamed and kicked the head teacher who merrily swooped me up into her arms and carried me to my classroom, telling my Mum, "she is going to be fine Mrs W, off you go now, we will look after her from here". She gave me "important jobs" to do, like drawing illustrations for a story for her small niece who was ill and she let me do it just outside the classroom away from the scariness of the class environment, but in sight of everyone. When I left to go to a different junior school to join most of my friends, she presented me with a small cuddly toy in assembly and said I should keep it to remember all the good times, and to feel brave about going to a new exciting place.

I think my head teacher understood transitions well. In fact, she wrote letters to me when she retired – and we corresponded well into my teens.

When considering what strategies need to be put in place, it must be remembered that the young children in our settings are not in a state of 'being prepared' for school or the next setting. There is a traditional perception that all the work done with children before they are five years old is done in order to get them ready for the next stage. But children are actually constantly acquiring new skills that will help them to deal with situations as they go along – they need strategies to deal with the here and now. One of these strategies is dealing with change. Transition between settings is just such a change.

It is worthwhile pausing to think about how you deal with change in your own life, and then reflecting on the observation from Brooker (2008) quoted in chapter one that children can experience more disruption and discontinuity 'than their professional caregivers have experienced in the course of their own lives' (Brooker, 2008, page 3).

There are then three key things to be aware of:

- The importance of understanding personal, social and emotional development

- The importance of understanding that we are not preparing children for school, rather we are giving them life skills for now

- The understanding that we do not all deal with change in the same way

Each of these factors require that teachers know the children in their care as individuals rather than groups. Although this might seem obvious, it is important here as the more that is known about the individual, the better able the staff will be to support that child and family. This is not as easy as it sounds, and this chapter aims to highlight how each of the three key points above can be approached and understood.

Understanding personal, social and emotional development

This understanding must underpin everything that is planned for within settings. Each of the British curriculum documents states that it is important for children to feel safe and to have their physical and emotional needs catered for.

Over recent years the wellbeing of children has been re-emphasised as of huge significance to learning. As chapter one has pointed out, emotional wellbeing is key to the Childcare Act and because of this emphasis is given to the 'emotional environment' in the Early Years Foundation Stage. If children are unsettled in any way they are not going to become effectively involved in their learning. This has been exemplified in the work of Professor Ferre Laevers. He writes:

> Children (and adults) who are in a state of well-being, feel like 'fish in water'. They are obviously happy. They adopt an open, receptive and flexible attitude towards their environment. A state of well-being results in a fair amount of self- confidence and self esteem, as well as a big portion of fighting spirit. People with a high level of well-being have the courage to be, and stand up for, themselves and they know how to handle life. They radiate vitality as well as relaxation and inner peace. The prevailing mood in their life is pleasure. They have fun and enjoy each other's company and the

things happening to them. They also have an unhindered contact with their inner selves: their own needs, wishes, feelings, thoughts... (undated text, Laevers, page 15)

Reflecting this statement on to the children at the beginning of the chapter illustrates how these children were not in a state of wellbeing because a school setting did not meet their needs in some way to begin with. Fortunately the teachers involved realised that something needed to be done. This work however was not continued throughout the schools in question. Laevers points out that:

A "person can only reach a state of well-being when he/ she is functioning. This person knows, so to speak, what he needs for himself, what he desires, thinks and feels. This implies that he can also allow negative experiences. Yet, these are of a temporary nature and do not upset the person. He can handle them. Because of this 'being in touch with himself', a fully functioning person can enter into optimal relationships with his environment. (undated text, Laevers, page 15)

It is just such "optimal relationships" that will support a child through transitions. The signs of well-being are:

- Openness and receptivity

- Flexibility

- Self-confidence and self- esteem

- Being able to defend oneself, assertiveness

- Vitality

- Relaxation and inner peace

- Enjoyment without restraints

- Being in touch with one's self
  (undated text, Laevers, pages 16-19)

Children can be assessed as to whether their levels of well-being are low, medium or high. If the level is low then Laevers states that children will not learn effectively. Children need to be involved in what they do, and they will only be able to do this if they are happy and comfortable and above all, 'actively involved':

Development can only take place when children are actively involved, when they are occupied with a high, non-stop degree of concentration, when they are interested, when they give themselves completely, when they use all their (mental) abilities to invent and make new things and when this gives them a high degree of satisfaction and pleasure. (Laevers et al, 1996, page 7)

I take the words 'actively involved' here to mean children are involved in decision making about their learning and where it takes them. Laevers sees the signs of involvement as:

- Concentration

- Energy

- Complexity and creativity

- Facial expression and composure

- Persistence

- Precision

- Reaction time

- Verbal expression

- Satisfaction
  (undated text, Laevers, pages 20-22)

Using these two sets of guidelines Professor Laevers and his team have developed the Leuven Involvement Scale for Young Children that can be used to look at aspects of behaviour and rate levels of involvement against a five point scale:

- Scale rate 1: no activity

- Scale rate 2: frequently interrupted activity

- Scale rate 3: more or less continuous activity

- Scale rate 4: activity with intense moments

- Scale rate 5: sustained intense activity

These two crucial process indicators of quality in education can be shown to impact on the process of learning in diagram 1.

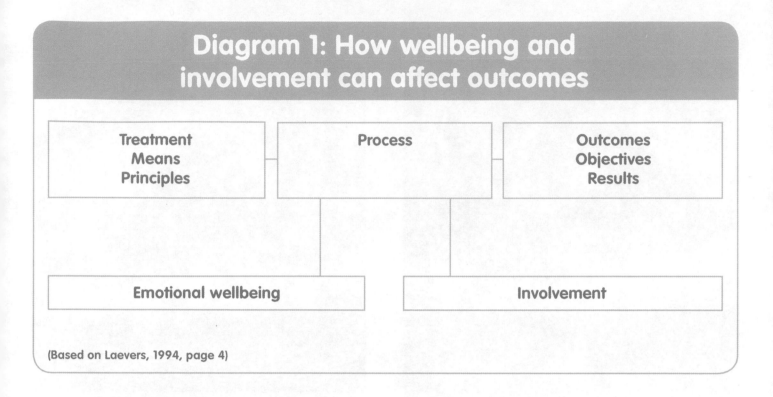

Diagram 1: How wellbeing and involvement can affect outcomes

Treatment Means Principles	Process	Outcomes Objectives Results

Emotional wellbeing	Involvement

(Based on Laevers, 1994, page 4)

Put simply, the first box 'treatment, means, principles' asks for consideration of what the setting provides through its vision, provision and practice. The second box asks for reflection on the processes and procedures in the setting and whether these are appropriate. The third box looks at whether the outcomes are those we would wish for, and if they are not, then we must reflect on the process. What this means is, that without emotional wellbeing there will be no involvement in whatever process is required so the outcomes and results will not be as good as they might be.

Once a child, group or class has been assessed against this, the adults have a starting point to support improved outcomes where necessary.

The numbers in the Leuven scales do not rate or grade a child as in a test. They show the adult where there are issues to address and what the next steps might be. The results will help to:

● Identify children who need extra care

● Observe more closely and analyse children's problems

● Set out goals for actions and possible interventions (undated text, Laevers, page 22)

The next section looks at how to understand the word 'learning' in a useful and supportive way, when thinking about transition situations.

Giving children the life skills for now

Professor Laevers identified that if children have a positive sense of wellbeing they will be better able to become involved in their learning. However, this does not mean that this 'learning' is to be defined in a narrow curriculum context of reading and writing. It is important to consider the twin terms 'care' and 'education'. This is because over the years these terms, and the meanings they carry, have become seen as separate. For example, childminders, playgroups and pre-schools have been seen as offering care, particularly if they enable parents to return to work, whilst schools are seen to be offering 'education'. The titles of the various groups that children may attend before they are five could be seen to suggest that no 'learning' in a 'school' sense happens in these settings. This leaves all those working with children under five in a potentially ambiguous situation. Now, however, the documents and guidance can be interpreted as leading all early years settings, including childminders, to focus more on 'school' learning 'particularly literacy and numeracy'. In this way 'top down' pressure to concentrate on these areas of learning is felt by those working with young children and the personal and emotional wellbeing of individuals is in danger of being lost. Dahlberg and Moss (2005) suggest that the term 'pedagogy' is a better way of describing the relationship between care and education because it "encompasses

A sense of wellbeing will allow concentration on a task

Learning for all aspects of life

learning and caring within a broad concern with all aspects of life" (Dahlberg and Moss, 2005, page 91). Their useful definition goes on to say – "preschools (or schools) might be understood as spaces in civil society where children and adults can engage together in a potentially wide range of possibilities" (Dahlberg and Moss, 2005, page 91). One of these possibilities is education. This is a helpful definition in the context of thinking about emotional wellbeing and the effects of transition and change because it allows us to focus more broadly on these issues and not feel constrained by a subject based curriculum and more formalised 'learning'.

Once we can see education, in its formal sense, as just one strand of what is done in early years settings, then the way is clear to address the needs of individuals. This thinking is also clear in The Early Years Foundation Stage (DCSF, 2008) where the 'Areas of Learning and Development' are included as section 4.4 in the Principle 4 'Learning and Development'. This makes the areas of learning only one sixteenth of the document, which largely focusses on the importance of supporting the unique children and developing positive relationships.

Taking a broader view of the opportunities both physical and emotional that are offered in settings means also thinking about how children are supported to develop the skills they need to manage their lives.

The emotional and physical environment

The environment that you provide for the children in your care is probably the single most important factor in determining how they, and the staff team, deal with transition. This is because the term 'environment' does not just apply to the physical space of the room, furniture, resources or outside area – it also refers to the emotional environment. In this section the emotional environment will be examined first, then how the physical environment can be supportive to it.

The emotional environment

This term is defined in the Early Years Foundation Stage (DCSF, 2008) as:

● The emotional environment is created by all the people in the setting, but adults have to ensure that it is warm and accepting of everyone

● Adults need to empathise with children and support their emotions

● When children feel confident in the environment they are willing to try things out, knowing that effort is valued

- When children know that their feelings are accepted they learn to express them, confident that adults will help them with how they are feeling
  (DCSF, 2008, *Principles into Practice Card 3.3: Enabling Environments*)

A clear, team understanding of the key person approach is crucial to creating an appropriate emotional environment. The Early Years Foundation Stage (DCSF, 2008) made this approach a statutory requirement in England. The Positive Relationships card 2.4 outlines this approach as:

A key person has special responsibilities for working with a number of children, giving them the reassurance to feel safe and cared for and building relationships with their parents.

The National Strategies published a document entitled Guidance: the key person in reception classes and small nursery settings. This defined the role as:

- A named member of staff who has more contact than others with the child

- Someone to build relationships with the child and parents

- Someone who helps the child become familiar with the provision

- Someone who meets the child's individual needs and care needs (e.g. dressing, toileting etc)

- Someone who responds sensitively to the child's feelings, ideas and behaviour

- The person who acts as a point of contact with parents

This paper identifies the need for children to have a key person to turn to at times of transition. It also identifies the possible difficulties of the role. Working in this way is only possible if the practitioners themselves feel comfortable in the team and understand their role:

In order to be able to respond sensitively to children's feelings, practitioners need to be able to be sufficiently open emotionally to be able to understand those feelings and yet also retain their own sense of 'adultness' in order to hold the child's distress. Sometimes adults can find themselves responding to children's demands 'in kind'.

Elfer and Dearnley researched emotional wellbeing in nurseries with a view to analysing the role of the key person:

Despite official endorsement of attachment principles in nursery work, these are often not translated into nursery practice. One possible reason for this is that staff training does not sufficiently address the personal implications and anxieties that children's attachments may entail for practitioners. (Elfer and Dearnley, 2007, page 267)

They identified four potential reasons for the "failure of implementation" of the key person approach even in nurseries that felt they were committed to it (Elfer and Dearnley, 2007, page 268). In summary these reasons were:

- It is difficult for many nursery staff to easily access continuing professional development. Many practitioners have not had the training to help them understand the key person approach

- The terms 'key worker' and 'key person' appear to be confused and used interchangeably. The difference being that 'key worker' is a social care term for someone who co-ordinates multi agency work, and a 'key person' in an early years context has a direct relationship with a particular child

- For reasons of child protection, practitioners may be reluctant to allow close relationships to form with children, particularly involving physical contact

- It may be perceived as "lower status" to work directly with the babies and young children, and "status" can be gained from doing more administrative and organisational tasks

Elfer and Dearnley's aim was to create a series of training sessions that would help staff to reflect on their own feelings at key times, thus giving them a greater insight and understanding of how the children in their care might be feeling. The key times that they chose to ask delegates to reflect upon included these four which are important for the theme of transition:

- Staying at nursery for the first time alone

- Attachment and the key person role

- Children's behaviour at nursery

- Team functioning

It was recognised that unless team members could identify their own feelings, understand these feelings, and in turn express them, they would be unable to effectively support the children in their care.

This chapter opened with asking you to consider times or situations in which you either feel comfortable or uncomfortable, and what the reasons for this are. Now would be a good time to do this in light of what you have read so far as this might have changed your thinking.

Attachment

Elfer and Dearnley noted that:

> Senior management must be committed if the organisational structures are to support reflective practice in a systematic and ongoing way. It needs to be recognised that resources have to be allocated for the time and facilitation for staff to think about and process the individual feelings evoked by their emotional work with the children. This involves an attitudinal shift too, seeing reflective practice as an entitlement of staff, both legitimate and necessary, if changes in professional practice are to be facilitated and sustained. (Elfer and Dearnley, 2007, page 278)

For example, the Study of Pedagogical Effectiveness in Early Learning (2007) states that effective practitioners are those who "Review, challenge and improve their own pedagogy through critical and informed reflection" (Moyles, 2007, page 57). But it is more than this, as Drummond points out:

> If the curriculum is infested with values, so too must be those who plan, implement and evaluate it. These conclusions are not confined to pre-school contexts… Understanding children implies understanding ourselves. (Drummond, 2000, page 103)

It is "understanding ourselves" that is important but at the same time difficult to achieve. It could be at this point that issues around attachment are brought to the fore. Adults in the key person role who may have had difficult childhoods or relationships themselves could find themselves in a difficult position with a child in their key group if they allow their own emotions to take hold. Equally, parents who may have had issues in their own childhood may find difficulties allowing another person to bond with their child. This is where the sense of "adultness" must come into play. Team meetings where staff can feel comfortable to share their feelings with each other

without being judged will enable the team to support children through transitions without their own feelings getting in the way. This kind of frank discussion will also enable the team to empathise with parents more.

How we speak to people

Part of making everyone feel comfortable at times of transition is how everyone speaks to each other, and whether people actually listen to what is said. Children particularly pick up on whether the adults around them are on friendly terms or not. This kind of thing may well mean making an extra effort on the part of the staff to make sure that every family is given time for friendly conversation.

This scenario from Brooker's work on starting school is a salutary lesson:

> The All Saints' ethos is one which overtly welcomes parents as individuals and includes them as partner-educators. Teachers are enjoined to 'ensure that the school's "Open Door" policy is fully implemented, that parents are made to feel important and welcome visitors, and that they are listened to, and their views receive a positive response'. But teachers are humans with their own personal history and ideology, so this is not as easy as it sounds.

> While Mrs Goode aimed, as she said, to 'work with' families in the ways they taught their children at home, in the majority of cases no dialogue existed from which she could learn what was going on at home. So even this inclusive and non-judgemental approach did not enable her to work with parents whose practices differed from her own. Becky's (the teaching assistant) wholehearted endorsement of the school's pedagogy (and her less sympathetic stance towards parents) would not admit diverse views about teaching and learning. Mrs Khan (the bilingual teaching assistant) as we saw was torn between faith in the traditions in which she was raised, loyalty to her employers, and a generous affection for all the All Saints' families, whatever their background.

> On a practical level it was not easy for parents' views to be 'listened to'. The school did not make provision for home visiting, which Mrs Goode in any case disapproved of, believing it to be an intrusion into the private lives of families; and no individual parents' appointments were offered before the child started school, or during their first term – not in fact until the end of the school year, after written reports had been distributed. Only those parents with the linguistic and social skills to engage Mrs Goode in conversation at the

start or end of the day were able to share information about their child, or to find out more about the classroom. (Brooker, 2002, pages 119-120)

It is easy to have policies and statements that say what we believe, but it is much harder to put the statements into practice without reflecting on ourselves first. It is good practice to state in policy that a partnership with parents is aimed for. This thinking will include allowing time for parents and teachers to partake two-way discussions, from which both sides take useful thinking. This will show in how the environment in the setting reflects the families in the group, and how the families feel when visiting the setting.

The physical environment

The wellbeing and emotional needs of the staff and children can also be affected by the physical environment. This is particularly true at times of transition. Imagine leaving your home for a weekend away, then arriving back late on Sunday evening to find that everything is completely different and all the rooms have been changed around and you had not instigated this. Now think about your setting:

- Walk into your room on your knees so that you can see what the children see. How does it feel?

- How does it reflect the interests of the children, or even of your team? Are the thoughts and ideas that arise reflected?

- How do you use the child-initiated episodes? If your children want to turn the role play area into a monster that they can get into, how can you help them to use, or transfer, the skills you've been teaching in a meaningful way?

- When you stand back and look at your environment are you happy that what you see reflects the children, or do you see predominantly adult influences in the furniture, resources and displays?

- Do children make their own displays?

- Do you change displays, alter the theme of the role play area, and change the layout of the room when the children have gone home?

- Are children involved in the changes that you make?

The children trust that when they leave the setting they will return to broadly similar surroundings, and be able to continue operating in a way in which they feel comfortable and secure. They need to know that they are supported by familiar adults, resources, room layouts and routines. These may be subject

Interesting resources at a child-friendly height

An interesting display for adults and children

to change for the photographers visit or a concert, but these transitions can be dealt with if the children are secure.

This same feeling of trust is needed with children when they move within or between settings, and every effort must be made to develop settings that offer some continuity of ethos and understanding so that when a child goes somewhere completely new there are still things with which they can be familiar.

In chapter four there will be an example of an audit that can be used to support reflection on the environment that you offer and how it supports the children in your care. This will need to be done honestly, and each member of the team should be given the opportunity to reflect and have their thoughts considered. This may mean a different approach to staff meetings. If all rooms within a setting do this, and settings that are linked to each other, for example playgroups and schools, share their thinking, then children will feel more secure when moving on.

We do not all find change easy to manage

Differing responses to change

The concept of resilience is important here because if we are resilient we are better able to deal with change. Schoon (2006) sees transitions as events that "require reorganisation at either the structural or functional level during entry into and exit from a particular state" (Schoon, 2006, page 26). She goes on to note how our individual characteristics allow us to adjust our behaviour to changes and variations in the patterns of life. As adults we have life experience upon which we can base how we respond in any given new situation. Consider moving house, or changing jobs: as adults we have all had previous life experiences that help us to assimilate these changes. Whilst these experiences might be positive or negative, we can all remember how we dealt with them and the strategies we used to help us move on. Children have not had the life experience to draw on and relate their feelings to. Whilst we cannot give them that life experience, we can make a start on supporting the development of strategies and thinking that will allow even very young children to be resilient and cope with change.

In order to support resilience it is crucial that each child and their circumstances are known individually. Not every child will react in the same way, or even consistently, depending on the situation. As Schoon points out, an isolated issue such as the divorce of children's parents, may not affect all children in the same way – it will depend on whether the child has "a life history characterised by multiple disadvantages" (Schoon, 2006, page 9). In this way

it is essential to be alert to each individual and their experiences, but equally not to be judgemental if these experiences are not necessarily those deemed acceptable by the staff. For example:

> A child raised by working class parents will not necessarily experience poor quality care-giving or scarcity of material resources. (Schoon, 2006, page 10)

So as teachers we must not make such assumptions. This has become known as the 'halo and horns' effect. We cannot judge a child or family by the way they look, or the background that they have, matching children to our personal picture of 'good' or 'naughty' based on our personal experience. If this kind of understanding is expected from the staff team, then it is important for that team to have an open and honest relationship with each other. This is something that needs to be cultivated.

If we are to avoid making assumptions then communication with parents is important at all times, but especially at times of change and transition. Some families have had particularly traumatic backgrounds before they come to our settings, but they do not always feel comfortable to talk about it. This is how they deal with change and it must be respected. For example, a setting did not know that a little girl in their care had seen dreadful things in a war zone until she started to play with a story box about soldiers, and act out some of the things she had seen.

Families may have different understandings of what each setting will offer their child; some may not understand the value put on learning through play as this is an unfamiliar concept to them, some may not have English as a first language, or may have just arrived from another country:

> The culture of the home is not hard for a child to 'learn', because it represents the only, and therefore the natural and inevitable, way to be. It consists of all of the ways of living, and systems of meaning, which prevail in each child's family. It is present in each child's experience and expectations of how people look and talk and act: the ways people behave, the things that are allowed and encouraged, and the things you are not supposed to do (Brooker, 2002, page 2)

At some point the child will find themselves in a different situation with different expectations – this transition will be made easier if we do not have preconceptions. Brooker (2002) points out:

> The 'ideological tradition', which assumes that it is natural for children to choose, play and display intrinsic motivation to explore, may pathologise children whose early socialisation has taught them to stand back and observe, or join with adults in their activities. (Brooker, 2002, page 166)

Questions to ask of your setting

- What are your admission and settling in procedures?

- What kind of welcome do your parents and children receive?

- How does your environment look? What kind of impression does it give? Is it warm and welcoming?

- How do staff interact with each other?

- Do staff make time to talk with parents and carers?

- Do the children see their parents sharing friendly conversation and laughter with practitioners?

- How does the environment in your setting, both physically and emotionally, support the children?

- Are the children happy when they arrive and when they leave? If not, are discreet efforts made to find out why?

The next chapter will look at case studies to exemplify how different early years settings support the children and families in their care at times of transition. Reflect on the key points below as you read each study.

KEY POINTS IN FEELING COMFORTABLE DURING TRANSITIONS

- Young children have not yet had the life experiences from which to draw strategies to support in a new situation

- Children are not being prepared for school, but for now

- Adults and children all need their emotional wellbeing supported in order to develop resilience

- The physical environment and the emotional environment are equally important

- Parents and families, as well as the different understandings they bring, must be respected

- Do we take the time to listen? And act on what we hear?

Chapter 3

Different types of transition

The aim of this chapter is to use case studies to illustrate how a range of people that work with young children manage transitions and support children and families at this time.

Whilst reading the studies in this chapter it is important to bear these points in mind

- How does each study show the use of the thinking outlined in the previous chapter?

- Do any of the strategies or considerations surprise you?

- What thinking can be taken forward into your own work and policy?

All of the case studies are from English settings and are therefore working with the Early Years Foundation Stage (DCSF, 2008), so all references to documents will be to the EYFS. The subjects were chosen for the quality of the work they do, so their examples will support work in similar contexts where the documents from other countries are used.

The next chapter will further inform thinking on the development of policy and how settings can develop their practice.

The case studies will be laid out in the same way:

- An outline of how each practitioner works based on interviews and time spent in each setting

- Specific aspects of transition pertinent to each study

- A reflection on how each practitioner develops the thinking outlined in the previous chapter

New situations can be daunting

Children need to gain skills for life

In this way each study will emphasise:

- The importance of understanding personal, social and emotional development

- The importance of understanding that we are not preparing children for school, or the next stage if they are already at school; rather we are giving children the life skills for now

- The understanding that we do not all deal with change in the same way

At the end of each study these points will be used as questions to encourage team discussions that may be the theme of a staff meeting, or as a basis for the development of policy.

Case study: the childminder

Childminders can often be the first carers that young children have away from the family. In this way they have many transitions to deal with, some more obvious than others. I am putting this case study first for this reason. Because it may be that being left in the care of a childminder is the first time that a child has been left with someone other than a family member, and for concentrated periods of time, it could be argued that childminders are best placed to model what Dahlberg and Moss (2005) describe as 'pedagogy' – "learning and caring within a broad concern with all aspects of life" (Dahlberg and Moss, 2005, page 91). Perhaps more than any subsequent provider, the childminder has more of an all round role encompassing 'all aspects of life'. This became clear through the conversation.

The childminder in this piece is female, so when childminders in general are referred to it is as female. However it is important to realise that there are many male childminders.

"The need to be proactive"

The title of this section is taken from the childminder's own words, and this study will show clearly how she continues to be proactive with all her families, as well as her own.

For the childminder in this study, her first contact with families is made through recommendation. After this the process of familiarisation starts. The first step is what she called a 'pre-questionnaire' – ideas for this will be included in the next chapter. The questionnaire went through several versions, as it is important to 'get it right'. The questions need to thoroughly support the childminder in her initial understanding of the child's needs, likes, and dislikes. For example, it is important for her to know about foods, allergies, sleep, and toilet training so that she can cater for the child's needs. Also of importance is to know the child's language, if English is an additional language, or perhaps pet words for certain things – for example the toilet, food or upset. What is absolutely key for this childminder is for her to be able to identify what she referred to as children's 'the moment of trauma'. By this she meant that crucial time when it is important to be able to spot when a child is distressed and know what needs to be done. It is also important to recognise other signals, such as when a child needs to sleep and the child's habits and comfort need to be understood. For example, when my youngest children were looked after by a childminder they were happier sleeping in a bouncing chair or buggy than being put down in a cot. In this way it is important to respect what parents include on the 'pre-questionnaire' and spend some time with them so that their answers can be elaborated upon.

Once the questionnaire is done and the child is ready to start, it is important that there are settling in sessions. In this case these involve the childminder adopting an 'open door' policy to parents. This means that they can stay for a while, phone, or pop in. Text messages are also useful to reassure parents. An important point that the childminder noted here is that that the parents need support through the transition too. Just as this may be the first time that the child has been left for extended periods of time, it can also be the first time that the parent has left the child. This can be compounded by the fact that the parent is returning to the work for the first time after maternity leave. Having spent so much time bonding with their child and meeting their every need, leaving them with another adult can be very difficult. One of the biggest issues is making the break, leaving the child and going to work. The childminder said she always makes sure that parents do not 'sneak off'. She feels that it is very important that parents say they are going and that the children have the chance to say goodbye and witness the parents leaving.

As the childminder gets to know the family well she feels that it is important to maintain open communication. At both drop off and pick up time must be made to have a conversation, and it is particularly good if both parents can be seen at the setting at times. It is good if both parents are involved, so that the child can see can see that everyone gets on, and the parents can see the environment the child spends time in and perhaps meet other members of the childminder's family and minded children.

The childminder has realised that the "reality of working parents is an issue now more than ever", she understands that more and more parents feel the need to return to work and as such she must empathise with, and understand their needs. This requires respecting their wishes, values and beliefs, even if these are not her own. She said that "the childminder understands". This understanding is on three levels.

The first of these levels is that the child's family is important and, even though the child is with her for several hours at a time, there must be constant reminders of family for the children so that they are reassured that their parents have not 'disappeared'. In order to do this she makes sure of these things:

- That she engages with parents every time they drop their children off. A key part of this conversation is to find out how the previous night has been – how has the child slept, and is there anything she needs to know.

- That there are books of family photographs for the child to look at.

- That she uses family names in conversation.

- That she takes an interest in and encourages conversation with the child about their family – every member of the family is important.

- She puts photographs on a secure site that parents can look at from home. In this way the parents and children can share experiences and the children know that their parents have an understanding of what happens when they have gone to work.

The second level that the childminder feels she must understand is that she is the link between the family and any other setting that the child may attend whilst in her care, for example a playgroup or school nursery. There is a need here for the childminder to be proactive as she is the main line of communication between the group or school, and the family. The use of names and photographs is key here to – pictures and names of the key people from the other settings are used to encourage familiarity. She feels that there is a "message here for teachers" as they need to be aware that, as they are not seeing the parents regularly, they need to take extra trouble to make links with them

as well as with the adults bringing the children to the group or school. It has already been noted that parents can need support with the transition between home and childminder – this change can be even more keenly felt when it is the childminder that has the experience of supporting the child through their first sessions at a new setting. It is very important at this time of transition that the new setting has a relationship with the parents, as well as with the childminder. The childminder in this case study started by talking about the links she has with the schools that her own and her minded children attend – she felt that it was down to her to be proactive and make the links. It is up to the childminder as the go between to establish the mood of the child, or if anything unsettling has happened, so that the child's feelings can be understood and worked with. In this way she needs to have established the mood of the child at the time of being left with her in order to inform the next setting, and when picking up the child at the end of the session the reverse applies – she needs to liaise with the key person in order to understand the mood of the child at that point and give accurate feedback to the parents. These two sets of people may not realise the impact they have on her role – there are transition events for the childminder here in that she must adapt to fit the needs of the child in her care as they move between her setting and another, then back to the parents.

The third, and perhaps the most important, level that must be understood is that what happens within the family may have an impact on the child. This theme came up in the interview when there was a recollection of a parent being ill for a while and the effect it had on the child. In these situations it is particularly important that the "childminder understands" and that the child feels "comfortable" to be left as they may be unsettled. Knowing that the childminder knew Mummy and Daddy well helped in this situation.

Knowing what happens within the family does not just mean supporting with difficult times. It also means understanding what expectations are made of the child at home – for example around self- care and eating. The childminder felt that it is very important to respect the wishes of the parents in these instances whilst at the same time supporting the child with what she called the "transition to self care". Children will be used to the routines around food and toileting that they have at home. To ease these transitions the childminder asks parents to provide food from home to start with and takes the parents lead in toilet training. This may not always be straightforward however, and she has met with conflicts between what is expected of the child at home and how the child acts in her setting. A particular example of this was with regard to eating – at the setting the little girl would happily feed herself with a spoon, whilst at home her parents fed her. The childminder worked through this through photographs of meal times and modelling mealtimes when the parents were present. It is important throughout that everyone must feel comfortable.

On this note it must not be forgotten that childminders often have their own children as well as those they mind. This was the case here. The childminder in this study felt that it is very important to explain to her child what would be happening and how routines would be different – there would be a transition for the 'home' child as well. As much as possible things are done on an equal basis this even includes each child having a 'talking book' that includes photographs and comments that they can all share.

All aspects of life

If we return to the Dahlberg and Moss statement that pedagogy is about "learning and caring within a broad concern with all aspects of life" (Dahlberg and Moss, 2005, page 91) we can see that this underpinning theme of 'all aspects of life' runs as a constant thread through the interview and it is clear that the childminder is more than a carer for the child while the parents work – there are many strands to the role.

Transitions identified

As she talked many situations where supporting transition arose in what the childminder was saying:

* For the minded children – from their home to the childminder's setting

* For her own child to understand that other children would be sharing their day on a regular basis

* For the parents to feel comfortable separating from their child

* Taking children from her setting to another group that they may attend

* Being the 'go between' making the transitions to different settings for the child and making links for the parents

* Supporting the child and the parents with transition in self-care. Particularly with food, ways of eating and toilet training

* Being aware of changes in the child's situation at home – for example the illness of a parent or the birth of a new

The childminder's own child must feel comfortable too

sibling – that will mean a transition for the child as they may experience change in their familiar way of life

* The child's transition to independence

Now use these questions to reflect on what you have read in this case study and in previous chapters:

* How did the childminder show that she understood the importance of understanding personal, social and emotional development?

* What examples were there of understanding that we are not preparing children for school, rather we are giving the life skills for now?

* What examples were there of the understanding that we do not all deal with change in the same way?

The key message from the childminder was that:

Time spent on transition is time well spent, the impact of quality transition goes mostly unnoticed as young people thrive. However, the impact of poor quality, ill thought out transition can have a life-long emotional impact on children that can haunt them throughout their learning life and beyond

Case study: the playgroup

"Our aim is to treat each child individually, do all we can to reduce anxieties, and make each transition a positive one for all involved." This case study naturally follows that of the childminder as links are often made between the two.

The playgroup is situated on a large estate and is very popular – it runs both morning and afternoon sessions and has a waiting list. Until recently it was housed in part of a school, but now that the school has had a children's centre built on to it, the group has completely new facilities. This has meant that the group has benefitted from both better surroundings and new resources. Being in a children's centre has also meant that there are now links to the Stay and Play and childminder groups, with some families using all three.

Being well established and in the heart of a large community, families are familiar with the group and the staff have known some of them for a while as successive children pass through. This obviously supports transition on one level, but each child is different. By knowing families in advance the manager can often know whether a child due in may have special needs or circumstances. If this is known prior to the child joining the group the families are invited into the centre to have a one to one to establish any requirements they may have. Generally

however the first meeting the manager has with a family is when the parent visits the group and a registration form is completed. This form is important as it is the first step made towards the staff at the playgroup getting to know the child and family.

Parents are given the Playgroup Handbook, which can be translated upon request. This is an important document as it underpins the ethos of the group. Below is an extract from the Handbook illustrating the ways it aims to explain in clear language the role and responsibilities of the key person.

> The playgroup operates a key person system, which means that you have a named member of staff assigned to your child. This is the person that you can tell your concerns to, ask advice from, and talk about your child to. The more information you can give us about your child, the more we can help and enable your child, and care for their individual needs.
>
> Key to this understanding is for all parents to fill in an 'all about me' sheet about their child so that the practitioners will know the things that will help the child to settle and things that will help them to know what to talk about with the child.

Once a child starts in the group the 'settling in' process is detailed in the 'settling in policy'. The aim of this policy runs: we want children to feel safe, stimulated and happy in the setting and to feel secure and comfortable with staff. We also want parents to have confidence in both their children's wellbeing and their role as active partners with the setting.

Staff at the playgroup aim to make the setting "a welcoming place where children settle quickly and easily because consideration has been given to the individual needs and circumstances of children and their families." The first stage of this is that the parents are asked, on a flexible basis, to stay for the first couple of sessions. They are introduced to their child's key person - this practitioner tends to be the one that the child warms to in their first session. During this time, the parent can stay apart from the child, but the practitioners encourage them to play alongside their children so that they can share the enjoyment.

Once the parents have left, and as with the childminder in the previous case study it is important that parents say goodbye to the child before they go, regular communication becomes important. This is done through phone calls, an open door policy, and regular sharing of the individual 'Learning Journal' of each child. This special book is used to exemplify the significant achievements of the child throughout their time in

The playgroup is a welcoming place

the setting. Everyone contributes to it, including the children and the parents – they are free to take them home to add to whenever they wish. For the children who are less settled, or who have additional needs of some sort, a 'home/school' link book is introduced. The manager gave an example of this when she told me about a family who shared their experience of making cookies by not only writing in the book but also smearing some of the icing sugar on the page. This kind of thing is important as it allows the key person in the group to know what has been important for the child at home, and therefore what thinking she can develop in the setting. Knowing that there are links between home and the setting will help both the child and the parents to feel comfortable.

The Playgroup Manager is also aware that it is not only parents that bring children to the group and their transition policy details how they deal with this:

> If a child spends time with a childminder, or is brought to the group by a childminder, nanny or extended family member, notes or phone calls can be used to pass on information to parents, as well as verbally through the carer. Appointments can be made by parents if they would like to discuss any issues, and/or the child's progress.

This is exemplified by the fact that:

> Parents or carers and practitioners work jointly on the child's learning journey, and it is strongly encouraged that information about the child's wellbeing is shared both ways regularly.

Once the child is settled at the group and the parents have left it is important that continuity is kept and the child remains comfortable. The playgroup team are happy for the children to keep their "special cuddly" with them. Children need to be able to understand when their parents will be back to collect them and the Playgroup staff uses a visual timetable for this. The idea of this is that each part of the session is represented by a picture and these are displayed in a row so that the children know exactly when each event is happening and can discuss with their key person what will happen next and what will be happening before their parents arrive. This is very reassuring and a lot more real than saying "Mummy will be back soon", as time has no real meaning to very young children. All procedures are explained to the children so that they all know why things are done.

It is important at the playgroup that all the children know each other and the names of all the children are used frequently so that the children know them. Photographs of the children are used throughout the setting showing them involved in the various activities and areas provided. Some of these are laminated in a book. Using photographs in this way is helpful when children come in unsettled for any reason. The parents and/or key person can sit with the child and look at the books talking about each picture and identifying people – this has a calming effect. All children come into the setting and go straight to the activities so that in this way everyone feels relaxed when they come in and parents whose children are upset for any reason do not feel under pressure to leave them in a hurry.

Building relationships with families and keeping these links going is very important to the playgroup. In this way parents are always welcome at the group and activities are shared. For example, a teddy bear goes home with each child in turn and the families write a diary entry for him, and families are included in the running of the group through a committee and by volunteering at events.

As with the childminder, the playgroup can be the first place that a child spends time away from the parents in the care of others. In this way there are some parallels. Key to this is the word 'respect' and both settings mention the importance of respect for the families. For the playgroup this is included in their transition policy:

> All families will be treated with respect, and their child's circumstances are always taken into account when deciding the best approach to take regarding settling in to playgroup or their next setting.

Both settings are aiming to support the child in becoming independent and able to operate away from the parents. Both the childminder and the playgroup put in important groundwork to prepare children for their next setting. For the playgroup this is outlined in the transition policy:

> When a child leaves, either to attend another setting, or to begin their school nursery or reception year, contact is made with the relevant setting. In some circumstances, staff from the new setting are invited to visit the child at playgroup, or a trip to the new setting is arranged for the family. As we are based at [name of school], children who will attend the school's nursery will be taken round to visit the nursery in action, near the end of the summer term, and the school staff will in turn visit the children at playgroup.

Information is passed on to schools in the form of the [name of local authority] tracker of achievement, including notes and reports that may be relevant. The child's learning journey however will be handed to parents when the child leaves. Parents are free to use these as a reference at the child's home visit with their new teacher if they would like to share their child's previous experience and learning in this form.

Transitions identified

Some of the transitions identified in this study have a parallel with those in the study of the childminder. This is because, to some extent, the situations are similar in that children may be separating from their parents for the first time. But what are the differences?

- When moving into the playgroup, children have a chance to choose the key person that they "warm to" – this person supports their transition

- Transition between home and setting

- Transition between childminders and setting

- Parents are supported with the transition as the children settle

- The transition of children into a bigger group

- The realisation that some of the children may be going through more than one transition of carer in a day. For example, from home to childminder to playgroup

- The transition to independence

- The support for transitions to the next settings

Now use these questions to reflect on what you have read in this case study and in previous chapters:

- How did the playgroup show that they understood the importance of understanding personal, social and emotional development?

- What examples were there of understanding that we are not preparing children for school, rather we are giving the life skills for now?

- What examples were there of the understanding that we do not all deal with change in the same way?

The key message from the playgroup was:

> "Communication and working together – listening to each other (parents, child, carers, staff) to find the best and happiest way forward."

Case study: the day nursery

"Centering everything back to the child."

The day nursery is based on a college campus and mainly caters for the children of students and staff. Their prospectus states:

> We believe that every child is unique and is a competent learner from birth and can be resilient, capable, confident and self-assured.

We are committed to developing positive relationships so that children learn to be strong and independent from a base of loving and secure relationships with parents and carers.

To this end it is important to the staff that child sees that their parents and their key person know each other and talk together. This happens at registration when the key person is introduced to the child and the parents – this meeting is held very close to the time that the child starts so that the child does not forget it.

The team has identified that the key to transition is that everybody has ownership of it. In this way they have developed *Induction Guidelines for Early Years Educator and New Parents/Carers*. This is a list of pointers to guide the initial conversation with parents. It includes the following areas that are then elaborated upon to give further information:

- Introductions

- Key person

- Settling in period

- Time keeping

- Purpose of cooked hot meals/snacks

- Appropriate clothing

- Records

Photos show parents that children are enjoying themselves

The child's key person is important

● Early Years Foundation Stage

This document has evolved through use, and is reviewed each year to see if it still serves its purpose.

Time is taken to be sure that parents are comfortable and their needs are also recognised and understood. The team have noticed that transition and settling in can be more of an issue for the parents, it has been noted that "parents can be upset by the child having grown" – it is a wrench for parents to realise that the child is no longer dependent on them alone. It is particularly difficult for a parent when a child settles in quickly as parents can be more upset if their child is not. Parents are reassured that there is an 'open door' policy, and they may also view their children through CCTV. Photographs and videos are also used to reassure parents that their children have enjoyed their day and did not continue crying. At the end of the session parents and staff have time to talk about the child's day.

For the day nursery staff the key person role is vital, (see chapter two page 21 for more on this role). They see the key person as pivotal in supporting the process of developing the child's understanding of boundaries, routines and procedures. The team work respectfully together to develop the clarity of the role of the key person as one where the child can see that "love

and comfort do not just come from one source". The staff have recognised that attachment, for either the staff member or the child, can become an issue, but they are secure enough as a team that they can discuss and address these sensitive areas if they arise. They are clear that the key person is not a "surrogate mum", and the key person focuses on the child and their family. The team were very clear that they are not seen as undermining the parents. Parents and staff have a good relationship of mutual respect – everybody is approachable and familiar. This is particularly important when children move between rooms as they get older. As there is much shared space, including the outside environment, and the staff are all familiar, the transition to a new room and key person is less scary.

The teams in each room of the setting have leaders who recognise their team's strengths – they encourage them to reflect on their own feelings and those of the parents thus developing empathy. Room meetings are held every week in order to plan and discuss children. Time is found in the day for this and the same team of people is used to cover the rooms so that the children's routines are not disrupted by unfamiliar people. A 'handover sheet' is used between the teams so that the transition is informed and any needs taken into account.

This sharing of information is key to the work of the day nursery. In the Spring of the year in which a child may

Children help to create their own learning journals

be moving on to a school nursery or reception, the team start involving the child and parents in preparing for the transition. They start to bring the name of the new setting into conversation, they also name teachers and show uniforms. They also introduce the children to the idea of taking books home to share like they will at school. Independence skills are also further developed by giving children messages to take to other rooms, or asking them to take things to other members of staff. Contacts are made with the new settings and the tracking work that the team have completed on each child against the Development Matters Statements (DCSF 2007) is sent on to support further planning for learning.

Transitions identified

What are the similarities between the playgroup and the day nursery? What are the differences?

These transitions were identified in the study:

- Frrom parent to setting

- Between rooms in the setting

- Between adults in the setting

- Between inside and outside

- Between the setting and school

- Do the day nursery staff deal with different transitions from playgroup?

Now use these questions to reflect on what you have read in this case study and in previous chapters:

- How did the day nursery show that they understood the importance of understanding personal, social and emotional development?

- What examples were there of understanding that we are not preparing children for school, rather we are giving the life skills for now?

- What examples were there of the understanding that we do not all deal with change in the same way?

The key message from the day nursery is:

"We understand that the key person isn't a surrogate mum. We acknowledge everybody's strengths and weaknesses, and we use our own experiences to reflect on how the parents feel. We can often empathise."

Case study: the reception class

"We like to meet the children and families before they start with us."

The reception class is in a two form entry primary school that does not have a nursery. This means that the 60 children starting in the reception classes come from a variety of different settings, including some who have been at home and not attended any groups such as playgroups or private day nurseries.

The team began to be concerned that this diversity of background would have repercussions with both the adults and the children. In any one cohort there could be children from:

- Playgroups in two neighbouring local authorities

- Day nurseries from the same local authorities

- Childminders

- Care from extended families

- Nursery classes in schools from a neighbouring local authority

- Homes where parents have been with their children until their start date at school

The experience of the staff showed that, although some children and families knew each other either socially or from other settings, the transition into reception was complicated. The school has two reception classes, thus meaning separating 60 children into two sets of 30, with two adults in each room. The diversity of background experience meant that, unless the School team knew the family already, mistakes could be made inadvertently. For example, a group of children who had been together at a local playgroup were split into the two classes with three in one and one in the other. The co-ordinator had used the local authority criteria for making class groups, but was unaware of the friendship groups she was splitting up. This meant that at the new parents evening where the teachers and parents met for the first time there was some upset when parents and children found that they had been separated from their friends. Though apologies were made and the situation sorted out, the reception team were concerned to make sure that it did not happen again.

The early years co-ordinator had already put a programme of home visits in place (see chapter four for advice on policy and procedures for these visits). These involved two members of staff visiting each child at home at a time convenient for the families. These visits happened at the end of the summer term, by which time the classes had been allocated. Over a three-week period, also in the summer term, the children and parents were invited to spend a session a week in their new classroom. Both these strategies had proved to be very valuable, but the problem outlined above showed that something more needed to be done.

The team were aware of the many settings that the children had previously attended from the forms the new families filled in on accepting a place at the school. The next step then was to visit the children in these groups. There were already some links with two of these groups as they were on the school site, but the rest had to be sought out.

The contacts made in this way were very useful and resulted in children from the feeder settings visiting the school for various occasions, such as assemblies. The only place where it was not possible to make a link was the school nursery in the neighbouring local authority.

Whilst the links made were very useful, they could not help with the problem of the reception class timing – for the first term the children attended only in the morning. For those who had been to full day care, or the school nursery in the neighbouring authority, the expectation of parents was that the children would now be attending school full time. This caused difficulties for parents and children alike at lunch time as staff from nurseries, childminders and relatives or friends came to collect children to take them on to another venue. Children who were returning to a setting that they thought they had left were heard to exclaim, "But I don't go there any more – I'm at big school now!", and they could get quite upset.

The only answer to this was to change the system so that the children would attend on a full-time basis from the start. This was done after much thought around appropriate provision for children who may not be used to spending a whole day in a setting.

Moving into year one

This had always been easier for the reception team as they were in the same part of the school as their year one colleagues. This meant that the children were familiar with the adults and knew where the rooms were. During the summer term adults and children moved backwards and forwards between the two year groups in order to develop this familiarity. Handover sessions take place at which learning journals and any assessment results, in this case the Early Years Foundation Stage Profile, are shared and any needs discussed.

The difficulties for the early years team and co-ordinator at this point are twofold:

1. As the children come from a variety of backgrounds and have not all mixed before they enter reception, it has been traditional to mix the two classes as they move into year one. This is a hard task as the two reception classes have established their identities.

2. The team are concerned that the learning experience in year one is more formal than their reception environment and that transition will not be easy for all the children.

At the time of this case study these two difficulties remained. Based on what has been discussed so far, what would you do to resolve these two transition issues?

Transitions identified

As children get older the transitions they make through settings begin to differ slightly. One of the most striking differences on entry to a reception class is the ratio of adults to children – this becomes one to thirteen. A very different situation for children who may have been in a much smaller group, maybe even one-to-one with a parent, relative or childminder. This means it is even more important for the transition to smooth meaning that all the adults and children can be relaxed and familiar with each other.

Other transitions outlined were:

- From day nursery to school

- From a school nursery to a different school's reception class

- From playgroup to school

- From childminder to school

- From home to school

- From reception back to day nursery in the afternoon

- From a full-time private setting to part-time attendance at school

Now use these questions to reflect on what you have read in this case study and in previous chapters:

- How did the reception class team show that they understood the importance of understanding personal, social and emotional development?

- What examples were there of understanding that we are not preparing children for school, rather we are giving the life skills for now?

- What examples were there of the understanding that we do not all deal with change in the same way?

The key message from the reception class was:

"Once we stepped back and looked at what we were doing, we realised that we were not doing the best for our children and families. It has been challenging to reflect on what we were doing, but it's been worth it. And we aren't there yet!"

Case study: the year one class

"Learning from the heart."

The year one class is in a one of two entry classes within the primary school. The class teacher had previously taught in reception at the same school and this challenged and informed her thinking when she reflected on how she worked in year one.

As has been seen in chapter two the understanding of a year one environment and provision has moved on since the development of a clear Foundation Stage in 2000, which subsequently became the Early Years Foundation Stage in 2007. It has been increasingly clear that children are still very young at the beginning of year one and may not all be ready to start a structured curriculum input. Moving from reception to year one made this very clear to the teacher in this study.

Her first task was to address those who had not yet achieved the Early Learning Goals. Having an early years background meant that she was familiar with the Early Years Foundation Stage Profile and was able to interpret each child's score in an appropriate way. This meant that she saw the areas of learning that she needed to provide and these were planned for. She also saw areas where provision needed to change for groups of pupils and was able to plan for these too. The teacher feels that, "Year one planning is now a bridge between reception and year one, whereas in the past year one and year two planning was identical."

Changing the way planning was thought of in year one meant a change in thinking so that opportunities could be provided for learning to be embedded. Learning intentions are planned for and then notes are made alongside these as the week goes on. This kind of observational assessment reflects the formative assessment of the Early Years Foundation Stage Profile and is used to inform the next plans for children.

Changing planning in year one also allowed opportunities for children to revisit ideas so that learning could continue to be embedded long after a lesson had finished. This then meant that the environment, both inside and out, needed to be reviewed to support this way of learning. A box of musical instruments is stored on a low shelf so pupils can easily reach them. One day the teacher observed pupils playing musical instruments and practising the learning they had been introduced to several days earlier in a whole class music lesson.

Activities encourage independence

Adults work alongside children to develop learning

During the week planning is annotated to identify notes on progress and areas of misunderstanding. Provision is then adjusted to support pupils with difficulties. The class teacher said, "When we identify pupils as having difficulties in a particular area (e.g. place value) we then try to plan for activities around the room to support those difficulties, e.g. ten pound notes and one pound coins in the role play area."

Key to this style of working is allowing the children the time and independence to develop their thinking. This means having an environment where children can independently access everything they need – for example glue, paper, scissors, materials, split pins, sellotape – without their having to ask an adult for it.

The key points for the teacher are follows:

- Activities planned for are more practical, and include the use of the outdoor area, role play area, art table

- Activities encourage independence

- Activities are planned to reflect children's interests

Observational assessment also means having resources that will challenge the children's thinking – there are baskets of items, such as musical instruments globes and map jigsaws,

that have a challenge card attached to them to encourage thinking. Children can use these at any time. Every day the children have class challenges that are regularly referred to and talked about – this results in a real sense of achievement, and every effort is valued. The children evaluate each other's work in a sensitive way using 'two stars and a wish' so that all children get praise and then a thought as to what they might do next.

The teacher has carried out her own analysis of how the changes she has made have affected the children and supported transition into year one. A striking thing is that boys are happy to sit and write because they are always writing for a purpose, often as part of role play. Boys even bring in writing that they have done at home – for example a book about dinosaurs. Also striking is that all the children are sociable and work together developing and negotiating ideas. There are usually at least two adults in the room and they are seen to be working alongside the children extending what is happening and making notes against the learning intentions. Having more than one adult means that the outside area can be used, and exploration and investigation continue out there. The team have ideas to develop this space as, at present, it is part of the main playground.

Because the children feel comfortable and they are given time to become involved with what they do they are happy

Different types of transitions

to cope with the routines of the room. If they have to attend an assembly or leave the room for any reason they know that what they were doing will still be there when they get back. If it is necessary to tidy up then this is done quickly and efficiently because everybody knows where things go and they appreciate the need to put things away properly.

Having thought about the transition from reception to year one, the teacher is conscious that the children will be making another transition into year two. With this in mind she has looked at how the Early Learning Goals are linked to the Key Stage One curriculum and includes National Curriculum levels in her planning: "We try to ensure activities will allow pupils to make progress and work at National Curriculum levels one or two." She has identified that the children are making good progress. Her words were: "And because of all of this the pupils are happier and make more progress and achieve more!"

Transitions identified

The transition into year one is the first time that children in English schools move into a different key stage. For the two years of the Early Years Foundation Stage they should be having a broadly similar experience that allows for continuity and progression. As mentioned in the previous chapter, studies have shown that there should not be a change to formal methods of teaching in year one as children are not always able to cope with such a different style of learning. This way of thinking is increasingly being implemented with many schools taking forward early years pedagogy with good results.

The transitions in this case study are perhaps less than in the other case studies:

- From reception into year one

- From the Early Years Foundation Stage to Key Stage One

In some schools there might be a transition from having two adults in the room in reception class to only one in year one – which can be very difficult for some children.

Use the following questions to reflect on what you have read in this case study and in previous chapters:

- How did the year one class teacher show that she understood the importance of understanding personal, social and emotional development?

- What examples were there of understanding that we are not preparing children for school, or the next stage, rather we are giving children the life skills for now?

- What examples were there of the understanding that we do not all deal with change in the same way?

The key message from the year one teacher was:

"The children and the adults are all so much happier now... there is a cheerful atmosphere. This is because the children feel comfortable and they are given time to become involved with what they do they are happy to cope with the routines of the room."

KEY POINTS IN DIFFERENT TYPES OF TRANSITIONS

- Reflect on how individual needs are supported when adults have taken the time to understand their interests

- In each of the case studies the practitioners involved realise that the children need strategies to deal with change as it happens, and that this support will benefit the children's wider learning

Chapter 4

Things to think about and do

The aim of this chapter is to support you in developing your own thinking towards how you might review practice, paperwork, policies, guidelines and your environment with a view to supporting transitions to, from and within your setting. Developing your thinking in this section will mean constantly reflecting on the list of qualities from chapter two:

- positive attitudes

- diversity and difference

- safety

- valuing individuals

- listening

- respect

- cultural identity

- physical and emotional wellbeing

- building relationships

- developing confidence

- feeling safe to take risks

- positive sense of self and others

- secure relationships

- autonomy

- independence

- positively affirming environments

A positive sense of self and others

Use the audit on page 40 as an audit to reflect on your thinking about each of these qualities.

Whilst some of this chapter may be directly reproduced to use in your setting, it is important that teams have ownership of their documentation in order that they understand and apply it. In this way much of this section will be guidance to be discussed and developed as a team so that it applies to individual settings and the ways in which they work. Whilst working through this section it will be important to remember these key things:

- The need to reflect upon current practice, without being unnecessarily critical or personal.

- The need to have a shared understanding of why policies and guidelines are in place. This means that these

Audit to support a review of thinking

Quality	Prompts	What we do now	How could we improve?
Positive attitudes	Do we all make time to smile and greet every day? Even at the end of sessions?		
Diversity and difference	Do we understand that this is not just about different celebrations and festivals?		
Safety	Do we discuss safety with the children? Do they understand why rules are sometimes needed?		
Valuing	Do we value what the children bring to their play? For example, super heroes and gun play.		
Individuals	Do we take in individual opinions or needs?		
Listening	Do we make time to listen to adults and children alike? And act on what they say?		
Respect Cultural identity	Do we respect families and their beliefs and values?		
Physical wellbeing Emotional wellbeing	Do we consider how families and children feel emotionally and physically? For example the agoraphobic parent? Do we make children sit cross legged even though it can be painful?		
Building relationships	How do we make sure there are good relationships within the team as well as with the families and children?		
Developing confidence	Do we share our thinking and feelings with the children so that they feel confident with us?		
Feeling safe to take risks	Do we give opportunities for children to challenge themselves, feeling confident that it won't matter if they fail?		
Positive sense of self and others	Do we spend quality time with all the children? And know each one well?		
Secure relationships	Does each child know who their Key Person is? Is that person reliable?		
Autonomy	Do we allow children to make their own decisions that we accept?		
Independence	Does our environment allow children to make choices?		
Positively affirming environments	Does our environment reflect what the children and families have brought to it?		

documents must have key messages that all staff members have a hand in developing even if this means reviewing them when there are new staff members. Or, if documentation is devolved from a central source, documents must be reviewed by teams so that they are understood and made pertinent to the local needs of specific areas.

- There is little value in having files full of long documents. They will not be read or useful. Paperwork that is not regularly accessed or used must have its value reassessed as it can probably be discarded.

- Policies and guidance documents should not be static. When they are used regularly with each new situation, family or incident, new thinking will be triggered. All documents should be dated in order that they can be reviewed annually, and amended if necessary. This will mean that staff members, even if not those who originally wrote them will maintain their familiarity with the thinking and have the chance to add their own.

How to use this chapter

This chapter works from the premise that an appropriate environment must be in place to support the wellbeing of both children and adults alike, thus enabling transitions to be less stressful than they might be. The first section is therefore devoted to considering what your environment provides – first by outlining three scenarios to inform a team meeting discussion, and then through an audit that can be done in your setting to help staff reflect on provision and what it offers both physically and emotionally. This section ends with a consideration of the emotional environment. Three scenarios are also included here to be used as a discussion point.

Once the environment has been reviewed the policies around transition and settling in can be considered. The second section of the chapter will consider what should be the key aspects of a useful document.

Because it has been identified that supporting families through transition is as important as working with the child, the third section of the chapter will look at transition from the point of view of the parents concerned. In this way it will consider the application process for settings, the first visit, and how parents can be involved in the setting.

The chapter ends with four scenarios to use as discussion points at team meetings:

- A little girl's day at playgroup

- A little boy's day at nursery

- The reception class

- The year one class

Although these are set in four specific settings, they can all be used by any team to develop reflection on transition.

The physical environment

Consider the following two fictitious settings.

Example: the private day nursery

On arrival the visitor is immediately made to feel welcome, a drink is offered and the adults and children all offer greetings and smile. The adults are all clearly relaxed with each other, the children and what they are doing. This shows in their responses to each other and situations. For example, they have recognised a need for rough and tumble play, but also realise that this has consequences so therefore needs some loose guidelines. In this way they have put aside a session each day where this sort of play can be enjoyed on the carpeted area. There are three simple rules: rough and tumble only happens on the carpet at the designated time and, if you join in you must realise that you might get hurt. If this sort of play happens outside the allotted time, thus upsetting others, the children involved are spoken to in a respectful way, "I'm sorry boys, please can I have a word…"

Although there is one child in the room who has recognised behavioural difficulties, this is not immediately obvious as his needs are catered for. This has put extra stress on the staff, but they are dealing with it gladly as they know it is helping the child concerned. The adults all work alongside and join in with the children developing ideas.

Example: the school nursery

In order to get to the nursery room the visitor must walk past other classrooms. There is generally silence and the children are seen with their heads down writing or reading at tables. If there isn't silence in a room, there is an adult shouting for it, or requesting it by blowing a whistle. On entry to the nursery room there are children to be seen wandering aimlessly whilst others are running around play fighting. The adults are standing by a unit talking to each other.

The room is messy, not because there are lots of exciting things going on, but because equipment has been misused. Resources are dirty and broken. Displays are tatty and old. Even here the adults shout to gain attention. The visitor is hardly acknowledged by the adult, but the children are thrilled to have someone who pays attention to them and joins in their games.

Pretend you are a stranger walking into your setting for the first time. What do you see, hear, touch or even smell? All these questions are important to ask yourself as you view your setting through fresh eyes.

Walk into your setting on your knees, at the height of a child, what do you see? Is it attractive?

Chapter two includes an overview of the work of Professor Laevers around wellbeing and involvement. As part of Laevers' work he also outlined ten action points for redeveloping a setting to support wellbeing. In summary these are:

- Rearrange the classroom in appealing corners or areas

- Check the content of the areas and replace unattractive materials by more interesting ones

- Introduce new and unconventional materials and activities

- Observe children, discover their interests and find activities that meet these orientations

- Support ongoing activities through stimulating impulses and enriching interventions

- Widen the possibilities for free initiative and support them with sound rules and agreements

- Explore relationships with each of the children and between children and try to improve them

- Introduce activities that help the children to explore the world of behaviour, feelings and values

- Identify the children with emotional needs and work out sustaining interventions

- Identify children with developmental needs and work out interventions that engender involvement within the problem area

Reflecting on these will add to your thinking about your environment.

The emotional environment

For the child and family new to a setting all the things mentioned above have a profound effect and leave a lasting impression. A child might take an instant dislike to a setting because it is noisy for example. We can all remember a time when we went to a new place but did not like it for some reason, but a very young child may not be able to express this. For the children and staff working there, many unintentional negative messages also leave a lasting impression and this reflects in the way they all behave towards what they do and each other. If these messages are not dealt with, then times of transition will be more fraught than they should be.

Before starting to consider supporting parents and children there must be a process of self reflection – unless our own feelings are considered it will be difficult to work with those of others. To this end it is important that meetings are held where the whole team can discuss and reflect upon how they help children to:

- relate well to other children and adults

- make friends and get on with others

- feel secure and valued

- explore and learn confidently

- and ultimately to feel good about themselves.
  (DCSF, 2008, page 4)

In conjunction with these thoughts think about:

- What makes you angry, anxious or afraid?

- The strategies that you use to manage and deal with these feelings so you are ready to be with children.

- What makes your colleagues angry, anxious, or afraid? Are they the same or different?
  (DCSF, 2008, page 16)

Enabling environments checklist

The below checklist is designed to help you audit your learning environment.

The emotional environment	Comment	Action
How do my daily routines make it possible for me to get to know and treat each child as an individual?		
How does my environment demonstrate to children that they are welcome?		
How well have new children come to terms with their feelings on admission? How do I know?		
Do we have a partnership with parents that is truly two way?		
How do the staff interact with each other?		
Do your staff make time to talk with parents and carers – do the children see their parents sharing friendly conversation and laughter with their practitioners?		
Are the children happy when they arrive and when they leave?		
What have I done today (this week) to help children be more aware of their feelings?		
Do we respect the feelings of the children?		
Do we respect the feelings of the families?		
How do my feelings affect how I interact with individuals?		
How do I interact with children? Do I get down at their level and give them a chance to express themselves?		
Are the skills of conversation modelled?		
Do children lead interactions?		
Is open-ended questioning used?		
Are children engaged in their play – can they approach an adult for support when necessary?		
Does planning reflect the needs of the children?		
The physical environment		
How are the children able to be independent? To make decisions and choices? How does the environment encourage this?		
Are the resources of good quality and do children value them?		
The routine allows children time to follow through their ideas		
Are the children involved in how the environment is set out?		
What can be seen that is child initiated?		
How does my room arrangement encourage children to talk together, share and co-operate?		
Is the building easily accessible?		
Is the security buzzer answered promptly and cheerily?		
Is it obvious to both adults and children alike that they are in the right building?		
If there is a reception area, how welcoming is it?		
Are all visitors greeted politely and asked to sign in?		
If there are toilets to walk past, are they kept fresh?		
If busy rooms are walked past, what image are they promoting?		
Is children's own work proudly displayed, or has it been adapted by the adults to 'neaten' it up?		
Are the displays at a height where the children can see them and become engaged with them?		
Is there only work by the adults on display? Why is this?		
Is everything clean and well cared for?		
How out of date are displays? Does anyone notice them anymore?		

Example: first day transitions

Sharing a quiet moment can help a child feel comfortable

A hurried transition

A mum rushes into the nursery. It is her first day back at work after maternity leave and she is running late. Her baby is six months old – he has not been to the nursery before.

When they arrive most of the nursery staff are in the kitchen area, either drinking coffee or making breakfasts for the children at the setting. One member of staff is in the room with the children – she is also welcoming new arrivals.

The new mum quickly passes her baby, his bag of nappies and clothes, and his special cuddly toy to the member of staff on duty. This practitioner is already preoccupied with a much younger baby who is crying as his bottle feed is being constantly interrupted. The practitioner now has her hands full with the new arrival. She barely gets a chance to respond before the mum has rushed off to work. The new child starts to cry and scream.

The first day at school

The children arrive in the Reception class of a school that has no nursery. They have come from various backgrounds – playgroups, day nurseries, other school nurseries and straight from home. The children and their parents come into the rooms and there is a happy buzz of chatter while the children find where to put their coats and belongings. The staff are moving around talking and laughing with parents and children, taking particular notice of children whose parents have been unable to stay, or who seem wary. After about 20 minutes the parents start to leave – the children hug them and wave. Staff are engaged in play with groups of children, but they also interact with the parents as they leave. The happy buzz of chat and laughter remains after the parents have left.

The first day in year one

The children and parents come into the room where the teacher welcomes them and asks the parents to leave. The children wander around looking for something to do. The teacher, and there is only one adult in the room, calls all the children to the carpet where they spend the next hour doing the register and the literacy text for the week. When they finally leave the carpet every child goes to their set place. The tables are set in groups and the children discover that they will always sit in the same place. After the children have sat at their tables for an hour it is play time. They all file out.

It is important that teams feel comfortable with each other and not threatened or anxious. Managers need to respect the feelings of their teams just as those of the parents and children are respected.

Reflect on the following example of first day transitions which illustrate transitions at different stages.

Whatever the setting that you work in, it is worth considering scenarios such as those given here as discussion points – perhaps as the basis of a staff meeting. Questions can be asked of each description as there are good and bad points about each.

Transition policies

When writing a policy it is important to remember that all staff must take part in the process so that it is meaningful. The whole point of this policy is to promote effective communication between all agencies involved in the transition – the parents, the child, the new team and any other agency that might be involved. There are many examples of policies on the internet and these can be used as a reference, but guard against copying these directly and filing them. They will almost certainly not be appropriate for your setting and this will be picked up at an inspection. It will also mean that the team will not be familiar with the contents.

When looking at transition do consider both horizontal and vertical:

- Horizontal transitions are those that happen throughout the day and week. For example, between carers, practitioners, rooms in a setting, different settings and different elements of the daily routine.

- Vertical transitions are those that occur as a child gets older. These will include all those above, but also transitions to completely different buildings with new people, longer hours in a setting, a higher ratio of children to adults and different routines.

- It must not be forgotten that both types of transition will have an effect on all the adults involved – parents and practitioners.

Why have a transition policy?

The aim of a policy is to be supportive and make clear the process and expectations that will make transition calm and successful. The document needs to be more than just a simple list of events that families will be invited to at the new setting, but it must not be so long as to be cumbersome and unintelligible. Nutbrown and Page (2008, page 131) remind us of the need for: "Close attachments and respectful sharing of information as an essential ingredient in the nurturing of a young child to ensure both consistency and constancy."

This means that a policy must contain carefully thought out processes that will support the team. Nutbrown and Page suggest a list of examples that can be used to focus thinking when developing a transition policy:

- How can Jenny's new key person really ensure she understands Jenny's idiosyncratic behaviour at sleep time?

- Will William be able to take turns with the tractor and will his new key person understand his interest in trajectory schema and his dislike of enclosing schema?

- Will Michael's new key person understand that he is not being 'naughty' when he gets upset at lunchtime if the gravy is put on his lunch, covering his potato? Will his new key person in the tweenies room sensitively support his preference to pour the gravy himself just the way he likes it, next to the vegetables?

They continue:

> This is not about children being 'fussy' or 'difficult', or even 'spoiled'. The adults in any organisation need to plan for these periods of transition with the utmost integrity and sensitivity to ensure that the idiosyncrasies of little children are understood. (Nutbrown and Page, 2008, page 133)

A vision for your transition policy

All this means that when writing a transition policy the aims must be clear – these will be underpinned by the philosophy of the setting. In this way a policy document could open with the vision of the setting followed by a list of aims. A good opening statement might run:

> At Nursery X we want our children and families to feel respected, happy, secure and settled. We believe that every child is unique and we strive to develop each child to their fullest potential.

> In order to do this we will work in partnership with all our families so that we all contribute to the child's learning and development and thinking is shared.

It is important for us as a team that we all work together with mutual trust and respect.

We recognise that transition, both in and between settings, can be a difficult time for all involved – this policy has been developed by our team in order to support us all through transitions and make them the best experiences possible.

This statement recognises that there must be mutual understanding so that the issues raised by Nutbrown and Page can be easily discussed and shared so that no situation is misunderstood.

The aims of your transition policy

The next section of the policy will be the aims. These must support the opening statement by considering everyone involved. These aims could include:

- To be sure information is shared in a two-way process

- To be sure that communication is always open and two-way

- To support continuity and consistency through each transition, whether it be horizontal or vertical

- To be sure that everyone feels involved in the process, including the child

- To be sure that everyone's feelings and thinking are respected and, when necessary, treated with confidentiality

It is important not to have too many aims – they must be clear and precise for all to understand. The opening statement and aims are the groundwork upon which the details of process can be based – they provide the reminder for all of the reasons why the transition policy is so important. Once the aims are stated, then the processes must be clearly outlined.

The processes involved in your transition policy

The processes will differ slightly depending upon the setting and the age group of the children moving on, however certain aspects must be key at all stages:

- There must be a sharing of information between all partners in the transition. This may be in the form of paperwork if the transition is a vertical one, or a conversation if the transition is one of the daily occurrences at the setting.

- What kind of paperwork is to be shared? This must be made clear.

- Children and families must be given the chance to visit their new setting if one is involved. If the transition is one of the daily ones, then these must be fully explained and their necessity made clear to all involved.

- Provision must be in place for children or families who may be particularly vulnerable – there must be a facility for working with other agencies involved with the family and confidentiality must be respected.

- The role of the key person (see page 21) must be outlined if the transition is within the early years.

- An outline of the schedule and reasons for the meetings that will be held to support the transition process.

Each setting will have its own processes that are unique to its locality and families. However, it can be expected that some type of individual record of learning will accompany each child if the transition is to a new setting – a 'learning journal' may even be passed on. This will support continuity and progression as the new setting can take the learning forward. A transition policy must contain the processes that are pertinent to each setting around the kind of paperwork related to the child's learning that will be shared.

Home visits

If your setting does home visits for each new child, then this process can be included in the Transition Policy. It is important that all the team are sure about why home visits are important and what they are, and are not, used for. Things to bear in mind include:

- A visit to a family's home is a privilege. To this end it must be done on their terms, at their convenience. If a family does not want a visit for any reason this must be respected. Perhaps an informal visit at a different venue may be more acceptable.

- Home visits must always be done in pairs. This is a safeguard for all concerned, but is also very practical – with

Food can sometimes be an issue

Parents need to feel comfortable

two adults visiting there will be time for play and conversation and for everyone to feel relaxed.

- A visit to a family's home is not to be viewed as a time for form filling or cross examination – always remember that some families will have had other agencies involved in their lives which may not have been such a pleasant experience. A home visit is in no way judgmental, and should not be perceived as such. Writing any kind of notes could be perceived as threatening. It is an opportunity to meet each other in an informal way, play with the children and feel relaxed in each others company. This kind of visit will enable parents to share things in confidence if they wish – knowing that there are no forms being filled in and judgments made. That is not to say that forms cannot be left with the parents to be filled in after the visit. Remember that visitors with clipboards are intimidating and this will damage any relationship.

- Think about how long each visit needs to be. It is important that these aren't rushed, but also that the welcome is not outstayed. The family must feel relaxed.

- Take a resource from the setting to share with the child. A story sack is a good idea as it is interactive and allows the practitioners to interact with the child, whilst the child becomes familiar with something from the setting.

Confidential information

A home visit can be a good time for parents to share very private information with you if they wish to. For example medical matters, special needs or family circumstances. This must be respected as confidential and any paperwork given must be treated securely at the setting – the information only shared with those who need to know.

There will often be times when a parent needs to share confidential information with a new setting at transition. If there has been a previous setting then this may come from the team there. If this is the first setting for a child, then there may be information from other agencies that is passed on.

Settling in

A key part of a transition policy will be a section on 'settling in'. This section moves the policy forward from everyone becoming familiar with each other and the setting, to the child actually being left in the setting, away from the family, for the first time. By now the parents and child will have met their key person and had a couple of visits, but it is important that the parent stays with the child for a while at the start. The length of this stay will depend on your setting and will be included in the policy so that everyone is clear what to expect.

This part of the policy could also include statements about how the setting will gauge that a child has settled – perhaps when they have formed a relationship with their key person and the expectations of parents, such as that parents must say goodbye when they leave and explain that they are coming back. It is also important that parents know that the practitioners will not leave their child to cry – if this happens regularly then the child will not settle. It may be that the child is not ready to be left yet.

Parent's perceptions of your setting

This section will consider how things look from the standpoint of the parents, and will be supported by examples from documentation used by the settings in the case studies. It will outline the registration process for settings, the first visit, and how parents can be involved in the setting. The perception of the parents is important at all times, not just at transition. It is very important that there is a mutual understanding between the families and the setting. Nutbrown and Page write:

> There is no substitute for speaking with parents face to face and getting to know them. Admission forms can capture only part of the picture when new families join the setting. It is worth considering different ways of gaining information. Talking with families who are already well established in the setting is one way of anticipating the needs of prospective families and how best to collect the information which may be needed in order to build a fuller picture of the child. Some basic information is required on admission but additional information (the fine detail) can add depth and context to a particular situation. Parents may not wish to share some information and will not always want practitioners to know things that they may feel will be used to make judgements about them. A feeling of mutual trust is crucial. (Nutbrown and Page, 2008, page 149)

Parent's perception of the setting has to be positive. Details such as how the paperwork for registration is presented can have an impact.

Review what is given to parents from your setting and ask these questions:

- How clear is the wording? Do parents know what information to include?

- Are there any spelling or grammatical errors?

- Has the document been photocopied well? Have sections been missed off? Is it straight on the paper?

- Is the document up-to-date? Does it need revising to meet current issues?

- Are you meeting the needs of your community? Are documents available in all the languages spoken in your community?

- Does the document actually tell you everything that you need to know about a child or family? Does it ask too little or too much?

A good registration document will enable the family and the staff at the setting to feel secure that enough information has been shared. A high quality registration form will complement the information given in the 'all about me' sheet that parents fill in that the start of the 'learning journal'. Some settings, such as the day nursery in chapter three, put together an attractive folder for parents which contains a list of everything they will need for their induction meeting as well as any forms to fill in. This is a good time to include a permission form for parents to sign to say that their child can go on outings, or have their photograph taken.

A positive impression can be given by both the presentation of the environment (see the enabling environment checklist on page 43), as well as the attitude of the staff towards parents as prospective customers. If the first meeting, or the induction session, is not a positive experience then, whilst not putting the parents off completely, expectations and relationships might be damaged. The day nursery in the case study (chapter three page 30) has developed a set of induction guidelines. This is a list of prompts for staff to use when talking to new parents. This opens with introductions of themselves and their colleagues, then continues with explanations of:

- The key person:
  - What it means
  - How it works
  - Confidentiality

- The settling in period:
  - Visits beforehand
  - Saying goodbye at handover
  - Phone number

- Time keeping

- Purpose of cooked hot meals/snacks:
  - Social
  - Varied diet
  - Check the menu board

An example of a registration form

All the information you give us is kept confidential and is to help us give your child the best we possibly can. Thank you.

Child's full name: _____ Male/Female

Date of birth:

Name your child prefers to be known by: _____

Name of parent/s with whom the child lives: _____

Address: _____

Telephone number: _____ Mobile: _____

If there is a parent who does not live with the child, which parent has parental responsibility?_____

Name of parent who does not live with the child: _____

Address: _____

Telephone number: _____ Mobile: _____

Does this parent have legal access to the child? Yes/No

Who is authorised to collect the child? _____

(We reserve the right to refuse collection by any unknown person if we have not had previous notification of any change.)

Please give the names and contact details of at least two emergency contacts that can be reached if you are unavailable. Please include their relationship to the family.

Name: _____

Telephone number: _____ Mobile: _____

Name: _____

Telephone number: _____ Mobile: _____

Medical information

Name of doctor: _____

Address: _____

Telephone number: _____

Are there any other professionals involved with your child?

Name: _____ Role/agency: _____

Telephone number: _____

Name: _____ Role/agency: _____

Does your child have any heath issues or allergies that we need to know of? _____

Please update us if anything changes.

Personal details

What is the main religion in your family?_____

Are there any special festivals that your child will be taking part in?_____

What languages do you speak at home?_____

Will our setting be the first time that your child has been part of an English speaking environment? Yes/No

Additional information

Is there anything else that you would like us to know about your child that will help us to get to know them?

_____

_____

An example of a 'me and my family' form

My first name is: _____

My surname is: _____

My date of birth is: _____

I am: _____months/years old

I have: _____ brother(s), whose name(s) is/are_____

I call him/them: _____

I have: _____ sister(s), whose name(s) is/are_____

I call her/them: _____

My home language is: _____

I also speak: _____

Key words I use:

When I need the toilet I say: _____

I call my comforter/soft toy/blanket: _____

I say: _____ for 'mummy'

I say: _____ for 'daddy'

My other special words and their meanings are: _____

I like to:

Play with: _____

Play games such as: _____

Look at books such as: _____

My favourite toy is: _____

My favourite song is: _____

Other things I like: _____

I don't like:

_____

_____

_____

_____

_____

_____

_____

_____

Meal times:

The foods I like are: _____

The foods I dislike are: _____

I don't like it when: _____

- Appropriate clothing:
  - Sensible, suitable clothes and footwear, depending on the weather – outside area is always open
  - Supply a spare set of clothes
  - Supply spare nappies
  - No jewellery
  - Everything labelled
  - Clothes may get paint on them, muddy etc.

- Records:
  - Accident book
  - Medication forms if appropriate or prescribed medication
  - Nappy or sleep charts
  - Progress books and meetings

- Early Years Foundation Stage:
  - Planning and themes on display
  - Value of water/sand/outdoor play/painting
  - Awareness that rooms are a learning environment and mobile phones should not be used

- Learning and achievement

As the child is settling the families can start to share in the process of creating a 'learning journal'. This document may be called by different names in different settings, but it will become a crucial link between the family and the setting, as well as showing the progress the child has made.

This will start with an 'all about me' page. This will give the new setting important information about the child's likes, dislikes and preferences and is helpful at transition. After this opening page to the learning journal, which can also be illustrated with relevant photographs, the child's time in the setting will be observed and documented. A good learning journal will contain a mix of long and short observations, contributions from the key person and other practitioners, the parents and other significant family members and the child themselves. All these contributions will create a positive relationship and mutual understanding between all concerned thus allowing any horizontal transitions within the setting to be smooth.

The learning journal will be the basis of the information that is used to track a child's progress against the areas of learning. In the Early Years Foundation Stage a child is tracked against the 'Development Matters' statements – this allows teachers to see the stage a child is at and what learning may be needed next. When a child moves into the next stage, which can be a different setting, this tracking will go with them so that the next set of teachers can take the learning forward. The 'learning journal' can be given to the family at the end of their time with a particular setting as a lasting memento and celebration.

Not all parents find it easy to be involved with their children's setting. This can be for a variety of reasons, but it must be respected, and we must not be judgemental. Involving parents and helping them to feel included does not always mean through writing, conversation and paperwork. One of the best ways I found to involve parents that I rarely saw was to involve them in making, and supplying resources, for story sacks. Whole families got involved with this, and children enjoyed bringing in the things that had been made at home. Another way of involving families who can not be available during the day is to have a teddy, or other toy, that is a valued member of the class and goes home to stay with a different child every night. My teddy, Edward, had some great adventures, and every morning an excited child showed us photographs, writing and drawings of what he had been up to. He often came back with some new clothes, books or toys that parents had put in his bag. The family's contributions to this were very valuable and also served to involve them in the class even if they could not come in themselves. Relationships like this are invaluable when thinking about transition.

Reflecting on everything considered in this book

To sum up the ideas discussed throughout the book, this chapter ends with four case studies based on real observations and experiences:

- A little girl's day at playgroup

- A little boy's day at nursery

- The reception class

- The year one class

These are to be used as the basis for team meetings. Whilst they reflect specific settings, the points and issues that arise are generic and will be important to consider whatever situation or age range you may be working with. Each case study will start with points to reflect on as you read, and end with questions to discuss. These will not be definitive, as many other points and questions will arise that will be specific to your setting and team- the discussions around these will all then lead to well-informed and shared policy and practice.

A little girl's day at playgroup

As you read, try looking at things from Nina's point of view (Nina is two and a half years old). Whilst we can never really know what a child is thinking, use what you have read in previous chapters about the emotional environment to think about what happens when Nina is perceived to have done the wrong thing.

Nina, her mum and her baby sister walk to playgroup three mornings a week – the baby goes in a buggy and Nina shares in pushing the buggy. Nina loves the walk to playgroup and the things they see on the way – they talk and laugh a lot as they go.

When they arrive at the hall the door isn't open yet, so they wait and chat with friends. The adults arrange to have a lunchtime picnic in the park after they have collected their children - the children are all involved in deciding what food should be brought.

The door opens and the playgroup staff start to welcome the families in. The children are all excited by the thought of the picnic later and they rush in chattering. Nina and two of her friends go straight to the home corner and start to gather

together cups, plates, cutlery and all sorts of things to play picnics with. The door to the outside area is open and they carry everything out in two or three trips. It has been raining overnight and, because the garden is shaded by large trees, the ground is still very wet. Right under the trees it is particularly muddy in parts. The girls had wanted to set their picnic up on the grass, but realising that it was too wet they set up on a bench on the patio area.

All the time they were setting up, Nina kept looking at the muddy areas under the trees. Several children were wearing waterproof trousers and playing in the mud. She was clearly distracted and losing interest in the picnic. She stayed there a bit longer, then she moved closer to the muddy area intrigued by a little boy. Although it was very muddy, the little boy was unperturbed and was driving a plastic car and interacting with other children. Nina turned and ran indoors to get some waterproof leggings.

When she came back out she ran straight over to the mud and sat down in it by the little boy with the toy cars. Nina joined in and they built up a series of 'roads' like a map. This game went on for several minutes and they were both absorbed in what they were doing.

After a while Nina left the cars and ran over to an adult to check the time with her. The adult looked down at her watch, then showed it to Nina. She liked the fact that that she had

Feeling relaxed outside is important

Working outside is important at any age

been shown the watch and pointed to it. She wanted to know what time they would need to go in for their snack. It was nearly time for this, and the adult told her that the team had liked the picnic idea so much that they would be having snack time on the patio. Some chairs and tables would be brought out. Nina then stayed in the area by the door – there was a table with puzzles on it and she started moving the pieces around. She wasn't actually doing a puzzle.

The time discussed arrived and tables and chairs were brought out. Nina was still wearing her muddy waterproof trousers, and was told that she couldn't sit on a chair until she had taken them off. However, she was very excited by the picnic idea so she went to the table where her key person had set up and sat down hoping nobody would notice. The rest of the group sat down round her and they all began to chat and enjoy their snack. Suddenly the child next to her pointed out to the adult that Nina had 'a muddy bottom'. The adult quite sharply asked Nina to walk round to her. Nina was very upset, but did as she was told. She stripped Nina of the dirty clothing, but said she couldn't sit down again until her chair had been cleaned. Nina was left standing for several minutes as the adult took the dirty trousers to be washed and then came back to wipe down the chair. She shifted uneasily from foot to foot whilst the other children finished their snacks and left their tables to continue their activities. When her adult returned, she was able to sit at one of the vacated chairs to finish her snack alone, while tables were wiped and moved around her. When she had finished she stayed outside, but did not go back to the cars in the mud where the little boy had recommenced the game.

For the rest of the morning Nina stayed outside, but well away from the mud. She sat on the patio and watched for a while, sometimes interacting with the adult who had shared her watch. She fiddled for a while with the jigsaw puzzles. Most of the time she was staring at what was happening in the muddy area. Her key person tried to interest her with an activity indoors, but she wouldn't go in. She wanted to stay where she could see the muddy area.

Eventually it was time for everyone to go in as the session was over and they needed to get ready to leave. Nina was reluctant to go in, looking over her shoulder at the mud several times she went over to the door and lined up with the others. She was in the way of the door opening and, when this was pointed out to her by an adult, she moved - this did not bother her. In her new place in the line she started interacting with the boy behind her – the one she had been in the mud with.

He had muddy water proofs from continuing the game. He waved his hands around describing to her what he had been doing. At one point she put the boys thumb into her mouth and sucked it - she didn't bite, but the boy interpreted it as such and called to an adult. Nina's key person came over and, without investigating what had happened, spoke sternly to Nina asking her not to bite. Nina tried to explain that she hadn't bitten, but wasn't given a chance to speak. She and the other boy involved went indoors and remained together through his taking off his muddy things and going to the carpet for a story and singing.

Nina was very engaged and close to an adult, not her key person, during the story, and this continued when they started singing. She continued singing *Twinkle, Twinkle Little Star* very tunefully and held the tune when the rest of the group had stopped short.

She understood the procedure of putting away their chairs when that followed and went straight to the right place. She then realised that another chair was actually in the wrong place and so she moved it. At this point the door was opened and the parents came in. Nina heard her name called and she ran straight up to her mum smiling broadly and rooting about in her mum's bag to see what had been brought for the picnic. Whilst she was doing this, her key person came over to tell her mum about the incidents with the mud and the 'biting'. Nina was unaware of this conversation as she was by now talking to her baby sister in the buggy.

Questions

After reading this scenario discuss what you and your team would do:

- How many transitions can you identify in this scenario?

- How would you deal with these transitions in your setting?

Have you thought about:

- Whether your rules and expectations make sense to the children? Do they understand why some things are allowed and some are not? Does the team understand the reasoning behind the rules?

- How do you and your team respond when a child is perceived to have made a mistake?

A little boy's day at nursery

As you read think about two things:

- How you develop a partnership with parents?

- What might Julie have done differently? What did you like or dislike about what she did?

Daniel is 14 months old. His day begins at seven o'clock with a quick wash and breakfast. The television is on and the only talking amongst the adults is the odd request to pass the milk, or butter. At 7.45am everyone bundles into the car and the little boy is strapped into his car seat. His soft toy comforter is still on the kitchen table.

There is a lot of traffic, so they arrive at nursery late. This means that mum rushes to unstrap the car seat while his dad keeps the engine running – they are both going to be late to work. The little boy's key person has already noticed that he is late and has been waiting and wondering about him near the door. This means she sees him coming so can go straight to the door to greet him. This is helpful for his mum as she can hand her son straight over to someone who is familiar and she knows he will be comfortable with them.

The little boy is hurriedly passed over to his key person with hardly a backward glance from his mum. The key person, we'll call her Julie, realises that things have been a bit frantic and that the mother is stressed, so she very calmly says to the little boy, who is now crying, "Say bye bye to mummy Daniel, and then we can go into the garden." They wave as the car pulls away with the parents waving from the inside.

Julie knows that Daniel's favourite place is the garden so that is why she started talking to him about it. They wave until the car disappears, then, with Daniel still in her arms Julie slowly turns away from the door. Daniel is still looking back so Julie gently continues talking to him about the garden as they walk towards it. She tells him who is at nursery that day, who is in the garden, which adults are outside and what new things are out there that he might be interested in. Gradually Daniel stops crying and starts to look ahead rather than behind. When they get to the garden Julie gently puts Daniel down to see whether he will be happy to walk on his own and become involved. For a few seconds Daniel hovers around Julie's legs watching the other children. Slowly he edges away and started walking around in the garden. To begin with he pauses briefly at various activities. Julie remains watching in the background just to be sure that he will be alright.

After a few minutes Daniel becomes particularly interested in the sand pit. It is a big one that the children can actually get in to. Daniel walks into it and sits down. He picks up a spade and starts tipping sand into a bucket beside him. Then he finds a small cup and starts to tip sand out of that into the bucket. At one point he appeared to be tipping the cup to his mouth as if about to eat some, but Julie stepped in and saw that the cup was empty. Knowing that Daniel had settled, Julie walks away to talk to another child.

After a while Daniel needed his nappy changed so he got up from the sand and went to find Julie. When he came outside again some shaving foam had been put into a builder's tray in the garden. He was very keen to put his hands in this, but was not wearing an apron which was required of the children for this activity and there didn't seem to be one close by. Julie wasn't nearby, so another practitioner carried him indoors to find an apron. He let this happen, but kept looking back at the garden and the shaving foam. They could not find an apron so they came back out. However, Daniel was not to be deterred from putting his hands in the foam. Julie came back outside and discussed with the other practitioner what could be worn to protect Daniel's clothes. Julie did not see the need for aprons to be worn with the shaving foam activity and she said so. Daniel snuggled into her legs whilst this conversation was going on. Then he saw another adult watching. For a few minutes he played 'peekaboo' with the other adult around and through Julie's legs. He was smiling broadly throughout this, and was distracted from the animated conversation about aprons that was still going on above his head.

A decision was finally reached that Daniel could wear all-in-one waterproofs, and some were fetched, though it was clear that Julie could not see the necessity. Daniel obligingly let them be put on, but became frustrated when it came to doing up the zip. Perhaps it had taken too long to put them on. He straight away put his hands in the tray of foam and completely covered his hands by sliding them backwards and forwards. He was standing alone doing this, although there were two other children sitting at the activity. A practitioner sitting with them started to include Daniel in the conversation they were having about the farm animals being buried in the foam. Though he was standing at the opposite side of the table to the adult, Daniel started to walk round to her, sliding his hands through the foam as she went. When he got next to the adult they had an interaction. Daniel started looking around as if looking for something. Julie was nowhere to be seen.

The adult at the shaving foam activity table needed to go indoors so she got up and started to walk towards the door.

Soft toys can be important

Role play can help deal with change

Daniel was watching all the while. At the door she passed Julie who was coming out to take her place. As soon as he saw Julie come out, he took his hands out of the foam and started whimpering to be picked up, trying to put his foamy hands on the legs of the practitioner. Julie told him that he was too messy to be picked up, but took his hand. It was clear that Daniel didn't want to play in the foam anymore. Julie wondered out loud whether it was because she had arrived.

Daniel still wanted to be picked up – he was clearly tired. Before he could be picked up however, he needed to be washed. But Julie could not leave the area so she passed him in to a colleague indoors. This caused him to fuss a bit, but he allowed it to happen. He then went back outside to find Julie where he got his wish and was picked up. However he was still fussing and Julie realised that it might be because he was tired. Julie called for his bottle and tried it, but he didn't want it, his dummy worked though. He was put in a bouncy chair that had been brought out, and gently rocked. He went to sleep very quickly - Julie remarked to a passing colleague how unusual it was for him to have a morning sleep.

Ten minutes later Daniel woke holding out his arms and screaming "Bah, Bah" – his way of saying 'bear', his soft toy comforter which had been left behind in the rush that morning. Until that moment no one had noticed its absence. Julie took him from his chair and sat him on her lap. He remained very upset – now that he had realised that Bah was not with him he was taking it badly.

As it was nearly lunchtime, Julie hoped that this might distract Daniel. She took him indoors so that he could see the preparations being made. He wandered around picking things up and putting them down – now that he had realised 'Bah' wasn't around he couldn't settle into anything and he was sobbing quietly. Because Julie was helping with the lunch preparations she wasn't always in sight, and by now no-one else would do for Daniel, even though other adults were trying to engage him.

Lunch was served, and Daniel went to the table where he sat with the rest of Julie's key group as the steaming bowls of food were put in the centre of each table. For a while he sat passively watching, or maybe staring in to space, whilst the rest of his group chattered round him. Bah would normally be with him in the chair to share his lunch. Every so often Daniel looked down for him.

Eating distracted him for a while – he always enjoyed this time with Julie and the others in his group, and he always ate well. Even though Bah wasn't there he still enjoyed his food and helped to clear away.

Normally after lunch Daniel would go for a sleep. Out of habit he went with the others to the quiet area, but he couldn't settle because he had had a short sleep in the morning and there was no 'Bah'. Seeing this Julie gently took him away from the sleep area and over to the cushions in the book corner. They sat down together and shared stories until the others had woken up. With a full tummy and a cosy cushion Daniel gradually gave in to sleep as the others were waking. Julie quietly moved away pointing out the sleeping child to the other staff so that they could all keep an eye on him. The other children didn't disturb him as they had seen children asleep on the cushions before.

Julie however, was in a dilemma. Daniel's parents like Daniel to have a sleep in the afternoon, but only a short one and no later than half past one as they felt this stopped him sleeping at night. Because of his stress over the missing Bah, he had already had a nap in the morning and was also now sleeping after the half past one deadline. Rather than wake him up and cause him further stress, and indeed problems for her too as she was about to be involved in a cooking activity, she decided to let him sleep on.

An hour later, the cooking activity was over and Daniel was still asleep. Julie had been too busy to notice. Other staff had checked on him, but not disturbed him. When she saw him, Julie panicked as he had slept late and for too long. It was only an hour now until one of his parents came to collect him – they usually came between four and five o'clock. She went over to the book corner and gently woke Daniel. As he woke he reached for Bah – suddenly remembering he wasn't there

he burst into tears. Julie picked him up and cuddled him, but the tears would not stop. As much as Julie tried to distract him, he wouldn't settle.

Just over an hour later Daniel's dad arrived. It was clear that Daniel had been upset and Julie explained about the missing Bah as she placed the little boy in his father's arms. She talked about the various activities Daniel had been part of, and how she had been distracting him from thinking about Bah. She also told him about the lunch Daniel had eaten and how he had enjoyed it.

Julie decided not to mention that Daniel had been asleep longer than usual, and twice in one day.

Questions

After reading this scenario discuss what you and your team would do:

- How many transitions can you identify in this scenario?

- How would you deal with each transition in your setting?

Have you thought about:

- How a key person in your setting works with parents? How do they communicate? Is it truly a two-way partnership?

Do you try to see the child's point of view?

Is putting an apron on always necessary?

- Do you try to see things from the child's point of view? For example, does it distract from spontaneous involvement in an activity to have to wait to put an apron on? Is there always a need for protective clothing?

The reception class

As you read consider what you have thought about in previous chapters regarding both the physical and emotional environment. How does the environment support the teachers' actions?

The doors open at nine o'clock and the parents and children come into the classroom where there are two adults waiting to greet them. The parents and children go through the room to hang up their coats and bags. When they have done this, they all come back into the room to self register by sliding their picture into a square pocket on a number chart that goes up to 100. A group of parents and children are laughing together as they put their cards into numbers in the 90's – will the teacher think there are more than ninety children at school today? Someone remembers that the teachers and the class teddy – Edward – also need to have their pictures put on the chart. Some parents have to leave to go to work – they have time to say goodbye to their children in a relaxed way though. The parents that have time know that they can stay until twenty past nine. During this time books are shared, games are played, and even some writing is done. There is a happy buzz of conversation with all the adults, including the teachers, involved with the children in activities.

At twenty past nine the children notice the clock and show the adults. This has become an exciting part of the morning, with children vying to be the first to tell the time, or let the teachers know if it is getting late. The parents start to leave and the children move to sit together on the carpet with their teachers. When the parents have gone the self-registration chart is then shared with the adults investigating who is in which number, where their cards are, and working out with the children actually how many people are really in class today. One of the teachers goes through the events of the day on a flip chart so that everyone knows what the schedule is, whilst the other makes a written observation of a child that has been of interest to the team. Once the order of the day has been established, the children move off the carpet. Both the adults have identified groups of children that they want to work with and they call them over. Everybody else settles down to doing something that has taken their interest.

At the moment the children are turning the role play area into a 'Garden Centre Pet Shop'. This was their idea and they are building and resourcing it. The workshop area of the classroom is busy with children making flowers in pots, and cages to keep animals in. A teacher's eye is caught by Alex who is on the floor with four large sheets of sugar paper – he is sticking them together to make a large rectangle. Whilst working with her group she keeps glancing over to see what he is doing. By now he has three other children working with him and they are making some kind of three-dimensional picture with boxes, tape and coloured card. The teacher starts to note down what she is seeing.

A few minutes later there are six children working on the floor. The teacher has finished working with her group and is intrigued to know what is going on. She gets up and walks across to see. Alex sees her coming and stands up proudly to tell her what they have been doing. On the floor in front of her is a three-dimensional picture of a rocket. All boys involved are very proud as both the teachers clear a space on the wall and find a way to fix the picture up.

Next it is time to share a snack. There is no need for any real tidying up – all that is required is a bit of space on the carpet. Everyone sits down and fruit is shared. It is time to share Teddy Edward's adventure. Every night he goes home with a child and the children hear about it the next day. Last night it was Scarlett's turn.

Scarlett goes to collect the bag that should contain the teddy, his equipment and the diary. She brings it over to the teacher and opens it up – as she looks in she bursts into tears. Teddy Edward is not in the bag! She must have left him at home. Everyone is immediately concerned both for Scarlett and the poor teddy who has been left on his own at home. What can they do to cheer everyone up? Connor suggests that they have a party in the afternoon and see if Scarlett's mum can bring the bear in. This is a good idea so phone calls are made and shopping lists written. A small group of children walk to the High Street to start the shopping with one of the teachers, Scarlett is in this group.

Over lunchtime the bear arrives back in school, and the teachers do the rest of the shopping. Straight after lunch, cakes are made, biscuits are iced and party hats designed so that, by the end of the afternoon a party can be held. Scarlett and Teddy Edward take pride of place and, before the food is started, she is able to do what she couldn't in the morning and

Things to think about and do

read out teddy's diary from the night before. Everybody claps and Scarlett smiles.

When it is time to go home another child is chosen to take Teddy Edward home. Everyone watches as he is safely put into the bag, still with his party hat on. Hopefully he will be back tomorrow.

When the children have all gone, the teachers notice that someone has altered the schedule on the flip chart. All the afternoon things had been crossed out, and 'party' had been written in.

Questions

After reading this scenario discuss what you and your team would do:

- How many transitions can you identify in this scenario?

- How would you deal with them in your setting?

- Would you do what the teachers here did?

- What would you do if the teddy was not returned, or some of his equipment was missing?

Have you thought about:

- Are your routines and planning flexible so that you can cater for unexpected events?

- Can children in your setting follow their own lines of thinking? Are resources readily available?

The year one class

- As you read consider how this study compares and contrasts with those given above. Although this is an example of a year one class, it could be any age group.

- How do you think Tommy feels? At the beginning of the day, then at lunchtime?

At nine o'clock the playground door opens and the teacher walks to her line of children. The parents have all moved away as they know they are not supposed to get in the way of the line. As the teacher leads her class in to the class room the children wave to their parents if they are still there. They have been told to walk quietly, so there is no talking. That is except for Tommy – it is his sixth birthday. He has his badges pinned on and is very excited. He wants everyone to know.

When they get into class the children hang up their coats on pegs that are right by the door, then they put their lunch boxes in a crate and their bottles of water on a unit which has a labelled space for each one. They go to the carpet for registration. Tommy is still bursting with excitement - he rushes up to his teacher to tell her all about his cards and presents. She asks him to sit down quietly and tell her later.

The teacher begins to call the register and each child says good morning, and whether they are having packed lunch, school dinner or going home for lunch. This takes several minutes. Once done the 'monitors' take the registers back to the office. While they are out of the room the teacher asks the children to spread out into a circle for 'literacy hour' – the monitors would then come back and fit in.

Today is Tuesday, and yesterday the class had started looking at the story of The Enormous Turnip. Each week there was a different story, and Tuesday was always the day that they acted the chosen story out. This meant that the children knew what was coming and, as they were moving into the circle they became quite animated, re-telling bits of the story. The teacher asked for quiet, and the chatter stopped.

Once in the circle, the talk about the story started again as the teacher had put a picture up on the interactive whiteboard. Tommy was poking the child next to him and showing him his badges. Again quiet was asked for as the teacher went over the story again on the board.

After this revision, children were selected to play various parts. They stood in the middle waiting for direction. Tommy had hoped he would be chosen, but he wasn't. The story started up again on the board. Everybody read it together and the actors played their parts. When this was done everyone sat back on the circle.

They announced that the 'literacy hour' was over and they were now going to do SEAL (Social and Emotional Aspects of Learning) time. This meant sitting in the same circle. Children were getting restless, especially Tommy who kept telling anyone who would listen about his birthday. He had been told to be quiet and sit still several times. Their SEAL topic today was to be around consideration for each other's feelings. The teacher had a story to tell round this theme. By now the children had been sitting on the carpet for over an hour and requests to go to the toilet were becoming frequent. Tommy made one last attempt to speak about his birthday and was told to be quiet again. He sat with his head in his hands looking at the ground until everybody moved off the carpet at the end of the story.

Before the children could move off the carpet the teacher wanted them to know what was out for them to do and who was going to work with her. She listed off everything and who must do what. The children got up and went to tables – some had forgotten where to be, or had not understood what was expected. A small group went to the outside door – there was an outside area for children to use – only to be told that it wasn't open that morning. This meant that some of the creative curriculum was unavailable as painting easels and role play were outside. The group wandered back into the room to look for something to do. They went over to the computers and stood and watched.

The teacher was working with a group on handwriting when she caught sight of the clock – it was time for assembly. This meant that everyone had to tidy up really quickly and line up, even though they had only just started whatever they were doing. Assembly lasted twenty minutes and was about 'special days' – Tommy smiled briefly. After assembly everybody went out to play for 20 minutes.

The teacher collected the children after play and they went back inside – she asked them all to sit at tables and take out their whiteboards and pens. It was time for handwriting practice. There was a brief time after this for everyone to 'choose' if they had finished their handwriting, and then it was time to tidy up for lunch. Children were sent to wash their hands as the tidying up was underway. When everyone was lined up the dinner lady arrived to take them to the hall. Tommy was glad to see her as he could talk to her about his birthday.

Questions

After reading this scenario discuss what you and your team would do.

- How many transitions can you identify in this scenario?

- How would you deal with them in your setting?

- What would you change?

Have you thought about:

- How much time do members of staff really listen to the children and use what they are saying?

- How are activities planned? How are the children's needs and abilities catered for?

KEY POINTS IN THINGS TO THINK ABOUT AND DO

- Review your environment – from the teams point of view, from the child's point of view, and from the parents point of view.

- Is your documentation fit for purpose? Review your transition policy, or develop one if none exists. Review registration paperwork.

- Do you carry out home visits? Reflect on how these are done – are they supportive or intrusive?

- Review how you work with parents. Are all families involved? Are some harder to engage? What could you do?

Different types of transitions

Sitting in a large group is a transition

The photographer's visit can be a worrying change

The aim of this section is to provide a list of different types of transition that may affect everyone involved in your setting. This does not just mean the staff and children, it also includes the following:

- the families,

- catering and temporary staff,

- placement students,

- visiting teachers of specialist subjects, and visitors who come to talk to the children about a theme – such as firefighters, police officers, nurses.

There will be others that you can think of. When reading this section it will be important to consider how these different groups of people might impact on your policies, and whether any new thinking may be required.

The table on page 61 sets out in no particular order of importance different transition situations, but simply with a view to inform thinking. These situations are all ones that I have either been involved in or have had related to me.

When discussing the list with a colleague they mentioned that although they had come across most of the transitions, they hadn't necessarily thought of them as such. For each transition it is important to reflect on how each individual child is supported, and the amount of parental support needed. All transitions do require some input from the child, and you should be aiming for each child to build resilience, so that when transitions occur, they can put in that vital effort.

Different transition situations

A different person bringing a child to the setting	Cutlery and styles of eating	Hospital stay	Parent losing their job
A different person collecting the child	Death of a pet	Illness	Parent working away from home for long periods
A parent helping in the setting	Death of a relative	Illness of a parent or relative	Photographer
A parent in the armed forces	Different clothing – perhaps a uniform	Inside and outside	Play time
A party in the setting – some children are terrified of clowns or balloons	Different moods	Lining up	School nurse visit
Absence of a familiar toy	Differing expectations of behaviour between setting and home, or even within the setting	More than one carer in a day	Seeing a show or a video – some children are terrified of certain stories
Absence of a friend	Divorce	More than one job in a day	Separation
Absence of a Key Person	Domestic violence	More than one setting in a day	Setting concert
Adoption	Expectations of independence. For example in dressing or eating where the same is not expected at home	Moving from a bottle to a cup	Sitting in a large group
Arguments – at home or in the setting	Fire alarms	Moving rooms	Sleeping in a room with others
Arriving from a different country or area	Food	New arrangements of furniture	Sleeping somewhere different
Assembly	Forgetting to bring a comforter	New child at the childminders	Staying over night with a friend
Being collected late	Fostering	New child in the key group	Table manners
Being late in the morning	Going full time from part time	New partner for a parent	Toilet training
Being new	Going to a party	New pet	Visiting performers
Birth of a baby	Hall time	Not having an adult to yourself	Visiting speakers
Brother or sister leaving home	Have a sibling at the setting, but being in a different room so not seeing them	Not using a dummy anymore	Weather – especially if completely unfamiliar
Changing setting	Having toys to play with when this is not something that is done at home	Outings – particularly if on public transport if this is unfamiliar, or to a destination that is unfamiliar, for example the seaside	
Changing times of attendance	Holiday	Parent leaving home	

Example: a playgroup's varied experience of transitions

Happy, relaxed children secure in their environment

Within the playgroup there are children who are each undergoing their own unique transitions. Clothing preferences can be distressing for children, and 'J' is the perfect example of this. 'J' has very strong preferences and genuine sensory issues. The two get a bit muddled, so the team just have to go with the flow. Thank goodness for leggings!

With all children we have issues with the transition from wet to dry, and dry to wet. Not just urine, but getting wet in the water tray etc. Some children really don't like this, whilst others don't care at all. 'J' hates the sensation of feeling damp, when neither wet nor dry, and avoids water play at school because if her sleeves get wet, she would need to remove the sleeves. She would also hate to have to wear something else if it did not feel right!

Again, some children don't mind wearing an apron, and some absolutely loathe it – and are even slightly afraid of aprons. Personally, I never wear protective clothing for jobs like gardening or painting - just old stuff, so why should I make a child stick a plastic, cumbersome overall on if they were averse to it?

A current issue the team face are parents who are involved in their children's learning. We are all for encouraging parents to be interacting and involved in the children's learning, but recently have come across a few who have just had way too much of it in some ways – they go to every session available in the children's centre and beyond, and the child's life is just so full of the adult's agenda, they have no breathing space – a little boredom would do them good! We had a child whose every waking minute was planned out and shared with his mum – so when he came to playgroup, he really expected constant adult attention the whole time – it took a while to wean him off! He resented it a lot at times.

The playgroup team didn't prepare well enough our children for our awards day – the morning children were totally thrown by not going straight to their coats after snack time. Some even cried! We had tried to explain earlier in the session, but the change was all a bit confusing. Now we have done it once, we can use photos from this one, and get the parents to explain it more – a few of the parents didn't realise what was taking place, or hadn't read the signs and letters, or forgot, so that did not really help!

Books and websites

Brooker L (2002) *Starting School: Young Children Learning Cultures*. Buckingham: Open University Press

Brooker L (2008) *Supporting Transitions in the Early Years*. Buckingham: Open University Press

Dahlberg G, Moss P, (2005) *Ethics and Politics in Early Childhood Education*. London: Routledge Falmer

Department for Education and Skills (2003) *Excellence and Enjoyment: A strategy for primary schools*. Nottingham: DfES Publications

Department for Children Schools and Families (2008) *Social and Emotional Aspects of Development – Local Authority Trainers Handbook*. Nottingham: DCSF Publications

Department for Children Schools and Families (2008) *Social and Emotional Aspects of Development – Guidance for Practitioners Working in the Early Years Foundation Stage*. Nottingham: DCSF Publications

Department for Children, Schools and Families (2008) Statutory Framework for *the Early Years Foundation Stage*. Nottingham: DCSF Publications

Department for Education (2010) *Practitioners' Experiences of the Early Years Foundation Stage*. Department for Education

Department for Children, Education, Lifelong Learning and Skills (2008) *Learning and Teaching Pedagogy*. Welsh Assembly Government

Drummond M J (2000) *Assessing Children's Learning*. London: David Fulton Publishers

Elfer Peter, Dearnley Katy (2007) 'Nurseries and emotional well-being: evaluating an emotionally containing model of professional development', *Early Years*, 27:3, 267-279

Laevers F (undated) *A Process-Oriented Child Monitoring System for Young Children*. Experiential Education Series 2. Centre for Experiential Education

Laevers F (ed) (1994) *The Leuven Involvement Scale for Young Children*. Leuven: Centre for Experiential Education

Laevers F (ed) (1997) *Experiential Education at Work*. Leuven: Centre for Experiential Education

Moyles J et al (2002) *Study of Pedagogical Effectiveness in Early Learning*. Norwich: The Stationery Office

Northern Ireland Curriculum (2006) *Understanding the Foundation Stage*. Belfast: CCEA Multimedia

Nutbrown C, Page J (2008) *Working with Babies and Children from Birth to Three*. London: Sage

QCA (2000) *Curriculum Guidance for the Foundation Stage*. London: Qualifications and Curriculum Authority

QCA (2005) *Continuing the Learning Journey*. Norwich: Qualifications and Curriculum Authority

Sanders D, White G, Burge B et al (2005) *A Study of the Transition from the Foundation Stage to Key Stage 1*. (DfES Research Report SSU/2005/FR/013). London: DfES

Schoon I, (2006) *Risk and Resilience*. Cambridge: Cambridge University Press

School Curriculum and Assessment Authority (1996). *Nursery Education - Desirable Outcomes for Children's Learning on Entering Compulsory Education*. London: SCAA and DfEE

Sure Start (2002) *Birth to Three Matters*. London: DfES Publications

The Scottish Executive (2007) *Active Learning in the Early Years*. Edinburgh: The Scottish Executive

The Stationery Office (2006) *The Childcare Act 2006*. London: The Stationery Office

Acknowledgements

My thanks must go to the staff, children and families of all the settings featured in the case studies for the support they have given me, the wonderful photographs and the helpful comments along the way:

- Debbie and Sian the Childminders

- Green Dragon Playgroup

- Wellington Primary School

- West Thames Nursery

The reception class case study is based on my own experience.

Particular thanks to Amy for being my proofreader and allowing me to use some of her 'ramblings'.